San Mateo County Parks

*A Remarkable Story
of Extraordinary Places
and the People
Who Built Them*

Michael Svanevik and
Shirley Burgett

San Mateo County Parks and Recreation Foundation
San Mateo County, California

ISBN: 1-881529-67-3
Library of Congress Number: 00-065588

Production of this book has been made possible under the auspices of the San Mateo County Parks and Recreation
Foundation, 215 Bay Road, Menlo Park, California 94025. Those interested in contributing to the foundation may telephone
executive director Julia Bott at (650) 321-5812.

Designers: Morris Jackson and Michael Benda
Publisher: San Mateo County Parks and Recreation Foundation

Cover photo: Copyright © 2000 by Down the Peninsula Productions. Touring on Sawyer Camp Trail, 1914. This photograph
was taken by photographer and inventor A.G.C. Hahn of Menlo Park. It was recorded in black and white on a four-by-five-
inch glass plate. The plate was subsequently hand-colored by Hahn and used as part of the San Mateo County exhibit at San
Francisco's Panama-Pacific International Exposition of 1915.

Back cover photo: San Mateo County Park Ranger Steven J. Durkin, in 1993, releasing a red-tailed hawk adjacent to the San
Francisco watershed near Sawyer Camp Trail. This photo was snapped by park aide Raymond Alvarez.

Preface

Schools don't offer classes in park appreciation. Perhaps they should.

Because, like fine art and beautiful music, great parks just don't happen by themselves.

All too often parks are taken for granted. People drive through or past them, often daily, usually giving little if any thought either to their very existence or to the tremendous service they provide for the community.

San Mateo County is famed for its many parks and for their unique diversity. The 14,000-acre system offers a distinctive park milieu for virtually everybody. Whether one is seeking solitude hiking amid the ferns through a redwood forest, or recreation in the saddle cantering along hilly horse trails, or windsurfing through the choppy swells of San Francisco Bay, San Mateo County provides appropriate venues. There are isolated campgrounds, picnic areas, fishing spots and kite flying fields. Each year over 2.6 million people visit the county parks.

In this county, so close to densely populated San Francisco and San Jose, there are broad sandy beaches where visitors may ogle harbor seals gamboling off shore in the shallow surf, and simultaneously, in the distance, see the spouts of stately California gray whales on their long migration between the Gulf of Alaska and Baja California. Along Sawyer Camp Trail, just minutes but apparently worlds away from a busy interstate highway, walkers sight deer, coyotes, and bobcats on a daily basis. Though roaming free, these animals have become so accustomed to regular visitors and feel so safe in their natural environment that they often seem willing to pose for photo opportunities.

This short book offers readers a basic overview of San Mateo County's parks and some of the colorful history of the growth and development of the Parks and Recreation Department. It is meant to be neither a detailed study nor a definitive statement of any kind. It is not a book on park politics or a discussion of park management.

Parks are an important part of the community and fill a very real need in an increasingly urbanized and industrial world. They are places families go together.

At the turn of a new century, however, the amount of tax money that goes to parks continues to shrink. Currently, just over one percent of the county's budget is allocated to the Parks Department. Unfortunately, this amount is inadequate even to keep up with inflation.

Faced with increasing costs and unpleasant budgetary realities, in 1998, the Board of Supervisors, following models established by the national and state park systems, approved the creation of the San Mateo County Parks and Recreation Foundation. The foundation's purpose is not to make policy but to help generate essential monies for the support of parks projects not presently provided for in the budget. "We realized we could continue to complain about the lack of funding or we could work on solutions," states Mark Haesloop, founding chairman of the foundation. "We are driven by the fact that people should not only enjoy their parks but help support them," adds Julia Bott, the foundation's executive director.

In the process of putting this book together, the authors have become more acquainted than ever before with the county's many parks, the dedicated individuals who run them, the administrators who make the system work smoothly, and, perhaps most important of all, many of the people who use them.

We like to view this effort as a first course, a mere introduction, in park appreciation.

Michael Svanevik
Shirley Burgett

San Mateo County, with a population of just over 700,000 residents, comprises 440 square miles on a peninsula directly south of metropolitan San Francisco. In area, San Mateo is the third smallest county in the state of California.

It is approximately forty-two miles long and its width varies between seven miles in the north and twenty miles in the south. More than fifty square miles of San Mateo County are in the Sierra Morena, a branch of the Santa Cruz Mountains running parallel to the Pacific Ocean forming the spine of the Peninsula. The average altitude of these mountains is 1,500 feet; at points they are twice that. The southern half of this range is heavily timbered with magnificent stands of coast redwood, *Sequoia sempervirens*, majestic Douglas fir, twisted tanoak and red-

A. E. Wieslander of the U.S. Forest Service snapped this photograph of virgin redwoods in the vast Pescadero wilderness, June 4, 1936. He was looking south across the ridge of the Sierra Morena from Jones Gulch.

PHOTOGRAPH BY A.E. WIESLANDER U.S. FOREST SERVICE

barked madrone. Steep slopes are cut by deep, narrow canyons where dense vegetation, rocks, and heavy underbrush at points make the Sierra Morena almost impassable. Murmuring creeks and streams trickle through most of the year.

Spanish explorers under Captain Gaspar de Portolá, who first entered the Sierra Morena from the coast in 1769, discovered not only a unique native population but a vast virgin forest, not yet scarred by the woodman's axe. The terrain was carpeted with lush vegetation and such densely towering trees that these explorers often found it difficult to see a hundred feet in any direction.

In late October and early November 1769, while part of the expedition camped at the base of the mountain on San Pedro Creek's estuary, from the nearby summit of Sweeney Ridge — since 1984 a part of the Golden Gate National Recreation Area and a national historic site in the northernmost part of the range presently separating the cities of Pacifica and San Bruno — Portolá's men became the first Europeans to sight San Francisco Bay. This amazing 700-square mile inland sea became the obstacle that finally checked the unflagging northerly march of the Spanish empire.

Along the county's east axis, between San Francisco and Menlo Park, at the entry to Silicon Valley, there are thirty-four miles of bay front. And, in the west, where heavy Pacific Ocean surf relentlessly pounds against rocky cliffs and broad, white, sandy beaches, the distance is fifty-five miles.

Though the county expanse can be easily crisscrossed in a matter of minutes by automobile, such radical geographical variations bring about dramatic differences in weather and temperatures. Simultaneously, while creeping fingers of gray fog, with accompanying cooling mists, invade like living creatures rising out of the Pacific, grassy meadows punctuated with wildflowers, just a few miles inland, are bathed in bright sunlight.

Perhaps, in part, because of the ease of access to its mountains, forests, and beaches, San Mateo County has developed one of the most varied and sophisticated park and recreation systems in the United States.

Custodians of the land have created more than a dozen separate county park units and historical sites in addition to hundreds of miles of mostly connected hiking, riding, and, in a few parks, biking trails. Many thousands of San Mateo County acres have also been allocated and preserved by the San Francisco watershed, the California State Parks, and the Golden Gate National Recreation Area for environmental study and recreation.

The variety of county parks is tremendous.

In Moss Beach on the coast, several miles north of Half Moon Bay, amid an intertidal region cut by dramatic channels and tide pools, students and casual visitors at the James V. Fitzgerald Marine Reserve, enjoy low tide, viewing one of the greatest concentrations of intertidal life in the

world in terms of numbers of species. Besides its abundant animal life, 186 species of plants have been identified.

Completely within the boundaries of the reserve, the reef is composed of soft shale or mudstone and is believed to have been created during the Pleistocene era between five and ten million years ago.

Those interested in the colorful nineteenth-century logging history of the county are intrigued by Huddart County Park, almost 1,000 acres characterized by steep forested slopes and deep shady canyons located along Kings Mountain Road east of Skyline Boulevard.

During the era of San Mateo County logging, between 1852 and 1860, five sawmills operated within the

Above: Woodside Store, located at the juncture of Kings Mountain and Tripp roads, as it appeared in 1950 before restoration.

Left: The rugged coastline between Half Moon Bay and Pigeon Point as it appeared in 1963.

3

AMPHITHEATERS OF ANIMAL LIFE

Black-tailed deer, especially active in the early morning and toward sunset, are sighted with regularity in almost all of the San Mateo County parks. This tranquil scene was recorded in Edgewood Park.

San Mateo County parks provide protected havens for the animals that inhabit them. Perhaps the most common of the forest creatures are black-tailed deer that frequent most of the park units. Deer feed early in the morning and later in the afternoon, often taking shelter during the heat of the day. Antlered bucks, seldom seen throughout the year, become prominent during mating season in the fall. Spotted fawns are born in May or early June.

There are also bushy-tailed gray foxes, skunks, gray squirrels and Townsend chipmunks. Twelve-inch long, dusky-footed woodrats build elaborate nests of debris and loose sticks, often six feet high and twelve feet across. These people-shy rodents venture out at night to gather acorns, berries, seeds, and nuts.

Though infrequently, weasels are seen carrying off hapless rabbits on brooding San Bruno Mountain. Campers in forest parks who do not protect their food can almost be assured of a visitation by black-mask raccoons.

On moonlit nights, mournful howls of coyotes, truly the song of the American West, punctuate the usual silence of the parks. Howls combine a quavering cry with a high-pitched yapping. Coyotes, which rarely attack people and will avoid them whenever possible, are members of the dog family and are the size and shape

PHOTOGRAPH BY SUSAN SOMMERS

of a medium-sized German shepherd. Grayish-brown coyotes with bushy, black-tipped tails are seen hunting in the meadows or along trails.

Also showing themselves during daylight in the parks, usually hunting for bite-sized rodents such as mice and gophers upon which they feed, are scrappy, pointed-eared bobcats, so named because of their stubby tails.

The largest wild animal remaining along the Peninsula is the tan, brownish-orange-colored puma or mountain cat. Unlike bobcats, the mountain cat is nocturnal and usually observed only at dawn, before the sun rises, or at dusk when the sun disappears into the Pacific.

These great cats stealthily wander through the twisted underbrush and tangled thickets along the ridges, north from the heart of the Santa Cruz Mountains. Only the luckiest people ever see them. The stately cats, known for long, gracefully curving tails, feed on birds, deer and other small animals. Attacks on humans by mountain lions in this region are unknown.

The vigilant will also identify many varieties of birds. There are flocks of quail, red-tailed hawks, great horned and the more delicate pygmy owls, turkey vultures, red-shafted flickers, band-tailed pigeons, various thrushes, doves, dark-crested Steller's blue jays and squawking ravens by the thousands.

boundaries of the present-day park. And while vicious scars left by the loggers have for the most part been eradicated by time, stark stumps of once majestic coast redwoods, albeit now surrounded by vital new growth, still punctuate this forest landscape.

Deep depressions on Huddart's open slopes bear witness to "skid roads," tracks made of logs laid transversely to allow teams of oxen to drag the mighty logs to the mills.

At the junction of Kings Mountain and Tripp roads, not far from the entrance to Huddart Park, is Woodside Store, one of several historic sites maintained by the San Mateo County Parks and Recreation Department. This structure is the first county-owned historical property. Built first in 1851, and rebuilt after a fire in 1854, for a time Woodside Store was the only general merchandising emporium on the Peninsula between Mission Dolores and Santa Clara. Six miles west of Redwood City, it became the heart of a thriving logging community.

While the great trees and the lure of the forest are ongoing attractions, joggers, walkers, bicyclists, and roller skaters unquestionably prefer the 6.2-mile Sawyer Camp Trail, a thirty-two-acre paved lineal park, not completed until August 1983, that runs between San Mateo and Millbrae along the shore of Lower Crystal Springs Lake, adjacent to 23,000 acres of San Francisco watershed.

Sawyer Camp Trail, with terrain reminiscent of Old California, was once part of the stagecoach route between San Francisco and Half Moon Bay. Crisscrossing back and forth over the San Andreas Fault, it winds through oak-punctuated grassy meadows, where wild orchids and other

SVANEVIK & BURGETT COLLECTION

Above: Motoring along what is today Sawyer Camp Trail was a special treat for travelers in the decade after the turn of the twentieth century. This photograph of an automobile party was taken in 1910.

Right: Believed to have been growing for more than six centuries, the Jepson Laurel is the largest tree of its species known to exist in California.

flowers abound in spring. There is a profusion of poison oak — "rangers' barbed wire" — protecting much of the trail. In the north, Sawyer Camp Trail enters a forest of trees and dense underbrush that provides users cooling shade throughout most of even the hottest days.

Along the trail is the imposing Jepson Laurel (Umbellularia Californica). Believed to be approximately 600 years old, it is unquestionably the most venerable and the largest laurel tree known to exist in the state of California.[1] The tree was already a century old when Columbus discovered America. A fence around the tree protects it from soil compaction.

Retired parks superintendent Bob Emert vividly recalls the protracted struggle to save the trail during the 1970s when it was threatened with destruction by the California Highway Department, then engaged in construction of Highway I-280. "It was one of the toughest negotiations I'd ever been involved with."

Sawyer Camp was an unpaved county road. On any given weekend, it would be blocked by thousands of kids partying. It became a serious law enforcement headache and

the sheriff really wanted it closed. Emert smiles remembering that the publisher of San Mateo's daily newspaper adamantly opposed opening the road to anything except automobiles. His opposition was based, among other reasons, he declared, on the belief that nobody would ever go way out there to use it. But within a few years, Sawyer Camp Trail, almost the

SAN MATEO COUNTY HISTORICAL ASSOCIATION

---

[1]*This tree was named in 1923 in honor of the noted California botanist Willis Lin Jepson. At that time, there was only one larger California laurel known. It grew near Cloverdale on the Russian River. That tree was felled years ago because it created too much shade on a hayfield.*

6

smallest of San Mateo's parks, became the most popular trail in the county, frequented by more than a quarter million people annually.

A few miles further east at the county's population center, at San Mateo, Coyote Point, a rocky, forested peninsula extending into the bay south of San Francisco International Airport, is 727-acre Coyote Point Recreation Area. Even though within hearing distance of a major freeway and directly under the landing pattern of the airport, it has become the county's most heavily utilized unit.

The park provides county residents rare public access to San Francisco Bay. Along the bay front are walking and bicycling trails. There is a yacht club with 575 berths. Not far away is a pleasant sandy, bathing beach where hardy swimmers frolic year-round in what overly enthusiastic local boosters once upon a time, advertised as the bay's "warm and salubrious" waters. Annually on New Year's Day, old-timers, members of the "Polar Bear Club," take the frigid plunge.

Strangely enough, adding to the widespread appeal of Coyote Point are the almost constantly blowing, often bone-chilling, off-shore winds. The wind makes this park one of the most cherished sites along the Pacific Coast for windsurfing. Almost any afternoon, while 800-ton passenger jet airplanes rumble overhead in their approach to San Francisco International Airport, the bay in the area is often filled with hundreds of colorfully wet-suited windsurfers skimming across the choppy swells.

Coyote Point weather is odd. It is usually possible to know where people are coming from. On any given day during summer, South San Mateo County and East Bay folks

SAN MATEO COUNTY PARKS & RECREATION DIVISION

Rocky Coyote Point was once a virtual island separated from the land by a low marsh that flooded at high tide.

picnic there to "cool off." Simultaneously picnickers from North San Mateo County and San Francisco are there to "warm up."

Within the bounds of the recreation area is a pistol and rifle range in addition to the famed Coyote Point Museum for Environmental Education. The museum began in a humble World War II Quonset hut on the site in 1954.

A few miles south, along a meandering paved bay front trail running through grassy wetlands, running parallel to the

COAST REDWOODS (*SEQUOIA SEMPERVIRENS*)

Unique qualities of coast redwoods made them the target of loggers in the decades after the Gold Rush. While most virgin trees in the county were cut, many wonderful specimens remain.

Since the days of the California Gold Rush, those who controlled timber property possessed "green gold." Coast redwoods were especially valuable. The grain of the wood runs straight. It splits cleanly, doesn't warp and was in demand for all types of construction. Redwood was the best material known for water, wine, and other tanks.

Buildings in early San Francisco were constructed almost exclusively of lumber drawn from the redwood forests. Pilings for wharves and piers, creating the port upon which the city was totally dependent, were also primarily built of redwood timbers.

On main thoroughfares, beginning in the early 1850s and continuing for a decade, city builders drove piles deep into the mud and laid boards atop them. Roads became continuous floors of redwood planking, wide enough for several teams to pass conveniently. Planked streets, of which San Francisco had many, were put down at a cost of $70,000 a mile. Sidewalks, without which foot movement would have been impossible in wet weather, were redwood as well.

In that era before barbed wire, orders by the thousands came from all over Northern California for fence posts. Cattle barons Charles Lux and Henry Miller used San Mateo County redwood to build their first fence in the San Joaquin Valley. That fence was sixty-eight miles long.

For bridge pilings, railroad ties and telegraph poles, redwood was the product of choice. One author estimated that in 1881 alone sixty million feet of redwood were consumed exclusively for railroad ties and fence posts.

present San Mateo - Hayward Bridge, is a 4,000-foot-long section of the original 1929 span — the so-called San Francisco - Oakland Bay Toll Bridge — that had been replaced by a more modern structure in 1962. San Mateo County purchased this three-quarter-mile-long segment of the old bridge (currently within the bounds of incorporated Foster City) from the State Department of Public Works in 1969 for a munificent $10.

Hereon, County Parks and Recreation operates the San Mateo Fishing Pier. Although presently closed to bring it up to code, the pier has become an increasingly popular site wherever confident anglers fish for bass, perch, shark, and other eatable bay specimens.

Much of the credit for establishing what ultimately became the San Mateo County Parks and Recreation Department must be awarded to Roy W. Cloud, County Superintendent of Schools during the 1920s. Cloud's position required that he make annual visitations to each of the county's many public schools.

In spring of 1923, Superintendent Cloud paid a visit to pupils at the one-room Wurr School, located in Harrison Canyon between La Honda and Pescadero in country thickly forested with majestic old-growth redwoods. Unquestionably, Cloud was enchanted. These trees, among the tallest in the world, rose to between 200 and 275 feet; some were twelve to fourteen feet in diameter. Beneath their spreading branches grew sword ferns, huckleberries, blackberries, tiger lilies, carpets of white-flowering oxalis and rare California wild azaleas. Each spring, wild mushrooms grow in profusion.

During the early years of the twentieth century, this section of Harrison Canyon, a roadside campground informally referred to as Camp Eden, had been a popular vacation spot for the small handful of county residents who knew about it. Though, even then, Camp Eden was surrounded by sawmills presenting an ominous threat to the magnificent groves of trees, some families had returned year after year to appreciate the wonders of nature.

While comprehending the majesty of these amazing trees and becoming enamored of wild azaleas then in blossom, Cloud became alarmed, learning from teacher Natalie Hanson that the forest had recently been acquired by the

Above: San Mateo County Superintendent of Schools Roy Cloud as he appeared during the 1920s when he first encountered the amazing redwood groves that became Memorial Park.

Below: Teachers and pupils of Wurr School, located in Harrison Canyon between La Honda and Pescadero, alerted Roy Cloud to the imminent danger that faced the forest.

Above: Timothy Hopkins of Menlo Park headed the advisory committee recommending that the endangered trees in Harrison Canyon be purchased by San Mateo County for use as a wilderness park.

Right: Lumber mills, characteristic of yesteryear throughout the Sierra Morena, still can be found in the forest. This particular mill was located in what is now the Memorial-Pescadero Creek Park Complex.

Peterson Lumber Company. Indeed, this magnificent sylvan sanctuary was slated for almost immediate destruction.

The ever socially conscious Cloud, saddened that many of California's most scenic wonders had already been despoiled, approached the San Mateo County Board of Supervisors, alerting them that the slope west of La Honda contained some of the finest stands of coast redwoods anywhere in Northern California. Though the county's population was then a mere 55,000, Cloud pleaded with the supervisors to save the forest by purchasing this amazing glen, ultimately 314 acres, and transforming it into a park to be protected for posterity.

Recognizing Cloud's sincerity and sense of urgency, the supervisors, with unusual haste, appointed a citizens' committee to evaluate the suggestion. The distinguished commission, which included Fred D. Lorton of Burlingame, William J. Martin of South San Francisco, Alvin S. Hatch of Half Moon Bay, and Josiah C. Williamson of Pescadero, was headed by Timothy Hopkins, distinguished scion of transcontinental railroad builder Mark Hopkins. In addition to being one of the largest landowners in Menlo Park, the younger Hopkins, a man with notable environmentalist inclinations of his own, was a trustee of Stanford University and had been responsible, during the 1890s, for laying out the town of Palo Alto.

Members of the committee inspected the proposed Harrison Canyon purchase, noting it was already surrounded by seven smoke-belching sawmills and that a virtual army of lumberjacks was relentlessly hacking down the giant redwood stems. Taking immediate action, the committee traveled along a circuitous, unpaved road to Harrison, the village nearest to the proposed purchase site. From there, they waded on foot into the sylvan forest, then

populated almost exclusively by black-tailed deer and other wilderness creatures.

Six weeks later, the committee was unanimous in its recommendation. They compared the rugged site to Big Basin in the Santa Cruz Mountains (California's first state park). Committee members determined that the acreage was one of the most beautiful natural park sites in California and recommended that the supervisors move to purchase it.

The property contained 200 acres of virgin redwoods and 100 acres of mixed timber with magnificent specimens of madrone and oak.

In August 1923, negotiations were undertaken with Edwin T. Peterson, owner of the property. Upon agreement, the supervisors agreed to pay $70,000 for the land, $35,000 at once, with the remaining amount due in December 1924. A special tax was levied to raise the necessary money.

In San Mateo County, as across the nation, citizens during the early 1920s were still recovering from the national trauma, sacrifice, and tremendous losses suffered by the United States in World War I.

Residents here, as those in thousands of other communities nationwide, wanted an appropriate memorial to those who had made the supreme sacrifice in war; fifty-seven San Mateo County residents had died in the line of duty.

Left: San Mateo resident Kurt Kuentzel attended the dedication of Memorial Park, July 4, 1924. His photograph of the ceremony is the only one thought to exist.

Above: San Mateo County Supervisor Thomas Hickey, one of the early proponents of open space, was heralded as "the father of Memorial County Park."

11

Every campsite at Memorial Park was occupied the night of the 1924 dedication. The Kurt Kuentzel and Frederick Loewe families of San Mateo were among the first to appreciate the tranquility of the park.

But until 1923, county leaders had consistently failed to agree on what form such a local war memorial might take. In March 1924, however, as the County Board of Supervisors was contemplating the purchase of the Harrison Canyon redwoods to be maintained as a park, Major A.J. Watson, commander of the San Mateo Council of the American Legion, suggested that the largest trees on the site be named for county residents who had died during the war. This idea met with the approval of the board.

Supervisor Thomas L. Hickey of South San Francisco, one of the most staunch supporters of the park plan, proposed that the new property officially be named San Mateo County Memorial Park. Thereafter, Hickey was known as the "political father" of Memorial Park.

Surveys were undertaken to designate likely camping areas. Waterlines were constructed. Platoons of workers, most of them volunteers from the American Legion, undertook the removal of slash that over the years had been left behind by tanoak operators. Meanwhile, county laborers began widening and resurfacing, not paving, Alpine Road leading from La Honda to the park entrance.

Ceremonies of such grand proportions had seldom previously occurred in San Mateo County. It was Independence Day, July 4, 1924.

Hundreds of automobiles and easily 1,500 people descended the winding, albeit newly surfaced mountain road from La Honda for the dedication of Memorial Park on Pescadero Creek. This was the first unit of what would ultimately be an extensive and sophisticated park system.

Elaborate preparations had gone on for weeks prior to the long-anticipated outdoor ceremony. It was, all later agreed, an impressive but simple and dignified dedication. For the occasion, a temporary platform had been erected in a clearing with a backdrop of towering coast redwoods forming a natural amphitheater.

County workers had speeded efforts to provide water and sanitary facilities to 300 campsites within the 312-acre grounds. Every camp was occupied on the night of July 4. Music for this somber yet happy occasion was provided by the Half Moon Bay Band.

All-day dedication exercises were carried out by the American Legion Post of San Mateo County. There was patriotic oratory by Morgan Keaton, Legion adjutant, followed by a dramatic reading of the Declaration of Independence by Judge Fletcher A. Cutler of Burlingame. Supervisor Hickey gave a stirring address and somberly read the names of fifty-two men who had died in the service of the United States. In Legion Flat, one section of the new park, fifty-two virgin redwood trees were dedicated in their memory.[2]

Later, with the assistance of San Mateo County Boy Scouts, small bronze memorial plaques, each bearing the name of a fallen hero, were reportedly placed at the base of the towering giants. Those gathered joined in singing "America" and "The Star-Spangled Banner."

The entire day was a patriotic spectacle. There was a mammoth roast beef barbecue, free to all participants, followed by open-air dancing. In the evening, those who remained clustered together around a blazing bonfire.

---

[2]A careful search of War Department records compiled in the year 1919 reveal that a total of fifty-seven San Mateo County residents died during the course of World War I. This number includes not only those who had fallen in combat on the Western Front but also those who had succumbed to Spanish influenza, many while still in training camps. Why the American Legion and Supervisor Thomas L. Hickey chose the number fifty-two has never been adequately explained.

Veterans of the Great War revived their favorite stories and again sang the songs they had learned while fighting on the Western Front in Europe.

"I expected a successful dedication but nothing so inspiring as the one that actually took place," declared an obviously moved Supervisor Hickey while the last embers of the bonfire were still glowing.

Memorial Park and the excellence of the work readying it for the dedication, provided primarily by American Legion volunteers who had labored side by side with county

Boy Scouts of San Mateo County were the first to make regular use of Memorial Park. For years the park was the venue for summer encampments.

Boy Scout activities at Memorial Park included swimming and lifesaving training in the icy waters of Pescadero Creek.

installation of electric lighting, construction of a rustic mess hall large enough to accommodate 200 scouts, sanitary facilities, a parade field, and wood platforms for tents. Pescadero Creek, which even on the hottest days is seldom warmer than an icy fifty-six degrees, was dammed to create a huge pool for boating and swimming. Sunday morning church services, for various denominations, were regularly conducted beneath the redwoods.

The first training session, for 157 Scouts and twelve leaders, opened from August 2 - 18, 1926. More than a hundred county residents drove to Memorial Park, August 9, to inspect this new campground. All expressed great satisfaction.

During summers, excited voices of uniformed youngsters echoed through the forest. Warren Swing, now retired and living in Walnut Creek, California, was among the first Scouts to camp at Memorial Park. "The program was run on a military schedule…and the bugler started the day with 'Reveille.' The cannon was fired, the flag was raised. Every Scout stood at attention by his bunk in correct uniform, with blankets folded precisely—ready for inspection," wrote Swing.

Swing, who has returned with his family annually to camp at the park, vividly recalls his days as a Boy Scout. In the mornings, there were educational programs for working on basketry, leather, and the preparation of merit badges.

"The campfire was the favorite event of the day with songs, stories and skits. Every evening the band marched and played a half-hour concert…. As 'Taps' sounded at the close of the day, once again all was quiet at Camp Pescadero under the majestic redwoods…."

employees, brought unabashed praise and enthusiastic comments from all in attendance.

But widespread utilization of Memorial Park was slow in coming. Not until two years after the dedication, in 1926, did the Boy Scouts of San Mateo County become the first organized group to take full advantage of the park for use as a summer training camp. At a cost of just over $5,000, they established Camp Pescadero on eleven wooded acres. This sophisticated undertaking included the

The San Mateo County Recreation Commission was not officially created until the adoption of the County Charter in 1932. The crash of the stock market three years before and subsequent Great Depression, in fact, gave impetus to the county's park development.

Increased national unemployment and a groundswell of unrest resulted in 1935 with the authorization by Congress of the Works Progress Administration (WPA). Proposed by President Franklin D. Roosevelt, this remarkable relief agency ultimately provided almost $11 billion nationally for beneficial public works. It was designed to offer minimal wages to individuals who would otherwise be on relief. Although Roosevelt's critics blasted the new agency as just another form of government dole, during a period of eight years, almost nine million Americans were given gainful employment.

In San Mateo County, young Ronald "Ro" Campbell, a Berkeley graduate in structural engineering and architecture, became the second full-time County Planner. He began without a staff and no budget but, along with the County Engineer, was placed in charge of directing and supervising all WPA projects in the county.

Under Campbell's direction, military-type barracks for 300 men were constructed and a WPA camp was established at the far west end of Memorial Park. It amounted to a virtual city in the forest. Among other structures erected was a huge mess hall, a hospital and maintenance shops, most of which were destroyed when the park was turned back to the county.

A major portion of the wood used in park construction was cut from the forest. Professor Emanuel Fritz, Chairman of the Forestry Department at the University of California at Berkeley, advised on the safest and most environmentally sound methods to proceed. "Sometimes you cut a redwood tree and you open up the wind pattern and others go down," stated Campbell remarking on the danger of haphazard cutting. Fritz pointed out which trees could be safely felled without destroying the character of the park.

WPA workers began ripping redwood logs into planks for construction of benches, trails, and bridges. Buildings themselves were prefabricated in Oakland and trucked to the park.

Almost everything that WPA workers did was accomplished by hand. Reverting to primitive lumbering methods not utilized in California since the days of the Mexican era before the Gold Rush, saw pits, six feet deep, were dug into the ground. Ten-foot sections of trees, stripped of thick bark, were rolled over them. Then, armed with sixteen-foot-long, jagged-toothed whipsaws, one worker stood atop a log and another below it in the pit, sawing the sections into planks. This process required two men laboring six weeks to create 3,000 feet of usable lumber. Perhaps 100 feet of square beams could be cut daily. Other teams of men set to work making shingles or shakes to be used on roofs of park buildings.

San Mateo County Planning Director Ronald Campbell directed all Works Progress Administration (WPA) projects in the county.

Adding to the male labor force at Memorial Park, were a large number of women, mostly runaway girls who had been forced out of their homes by lack of food and the general hard times. Federal authorities notified police agencies that such runaways should be picked up for their own protection. In secret, a camp was built at Memorial Park and an army-style barracks constructed for approximately 150 young women. Though substantiating evidence is not existent, it is believed the women assisted with cooking and washing responsibilities. Campbell noted that "it was necessary to keep the camp secret so as not to encourage other girls to run away." Several such camps were built at other parks in the United States as well.

Hundreds of unemployed during the Depression were hired by the Works Progress Administration. One of many county projects was transforming part of the untamed Pescadero forest into Memorial Park.

SAN MATEO COUNTY PARKS & RECREATION DIVISION

Retired Memorial Park Ranger Gary Woodhams, a lifelong resident of La Honda, who became a ranger in 1962, has nothing but admiration for the efforts of WPA workers. At Memorial, during the 1930s, Woodhams reports, they built the park and maintenance buildings, established the water and sewer lines, designated picnic areas, and laid out the campgrounds themselves. By the end of the year 1937, when the park was turned back to county control, WPA workers had completed the basic structure of Memorial Park.

Had it not been for federal monies made available for the WPA, development of Memorial and later Flood parks would have been long delayed. The thinking of the County Planning Commission and the Recreation Commission was to use all available money to acquire as much land as possible on the theory that, as the county's population grew, the land was going to disappear or become so expensive it would be unobtainable. "We went after land before the population sopped it all up," stated Campbell. "It was just to provide work that we undertook the most extensive development at Memorial Park."

Campbell frequently remarked about the genuine desire of people to find meaningful work during the Depression. Dissatisfied men, who were hired for WPA projects, often joked sarcastically about being paid simply to rake leaves. "We used to truck people clear over the coastside and hand-build walks and paths down to the beaches," stated Campbell. "We had a real hard time finding productive work for them. And these people did want to work. They really didn't want to stand around."

It was with this attitude that Ro Campbell began looking at a 21.6-acre piece of land in Menlo Park between El Camino Real and Bayshore Highway. "There were no plants whatsoever." Campbell later described the land as "a giant grainfield with some oak trees…." There he began to design a South County urban recreational park.

Campbell embarked on a personal crusade to persuade county officials to purchase the land, located on Bay Road between Marsh and Ringwood Avenue. Once an unused portion of silver king James C. Flood's estate, Flood descendants were convinced to relinquish the land for $400 an acre.

During the course of a year, devoted WPA workers transformed this windswept grainfield into what was later dedicated as Flood Park. Campbell recalled what he described as a thoroughly surreal working environment. Never had such an educated or more exclusive labor force been mobilized. There were real estate executives, lawyers, bank tellers, even bank presidents. "I can remember so many people coming to work in tuxedos," stated Campbell, "they'd sold all their other clothes. Tuxedos were all they had left because nobody was interested in buying them."

The store at Memorial Park, still in use, was constructed as a WPA project.

Phyllis Cangemi, a victim of Hodgkin's disease, led an effort to make Flood Park accessible for people with physical disabilities. In the process, Flood Park received national attention.

FLOOD PARK RENOVATION

At a cost of $800,000, Flood Park underwent a complete modernization during the 1980s. Today the renovated park is largely seen as the triumph of

Phyllis Cangemi, a disabled woman who became a Menlo Park resident in 1980.

Cangemi, a victim of Hodgkin's disease confined to a wheelchair or motorized scooter, approached the Parks and Recreation Division along with the San Mateo County Board of Supervisors requesting that they work to establish a facility that was friendly to disabled people. She asked that Flood Park be made into an international model for what could be accomplished. "The idea of doing something really wonderful captured their imaginations," stated Cangemi.

Restrooms and water fountains were especially designed. Heights of swings and benches were adjusted to safely accommodate the disabled. Wheelchairs could easily reach most of Flood Park's sandboxes and grassy areas. New benches were constructed with strong rails, allowing people to get in and out of wheelchairs. These are all types of details that often go unnoticed in other parks.

An obviously proud Cangemi notes that, since the park's modern renovation, it has attracted people from all over the world who visit to see exactly what can be done for people with disabilities.

PHYLLIS CANGEMI COLLECTION

Campbell designed Flood Park with early California ranch style buildings in mind. The style had been popularized by architect Cliff May in *Sunset Magazine*.

Working with almost no budget, Campbell reverted to the use of adobe, a combination of dirt, clay and straw mixed together with water and then formed into bricks to be dried in the sun. This was the primitive building material utilized by Spanish missionaries in the construction of all twenty-one Alta California missions. Once upon a time, ingredients had been dumped into huge pits to be kneaded by Indian laborers with their bare feet. They mashed the mixture until all lumps were dissolved and a thick pasty substance had been achieved.

In the twentieth century, Campbell modified this ancient technique employing a more refined and mechanized method. From a Menlo Park bakery near the park, he purchased a secondhand bread mixing machine. "Building a swimming pool was an essential element of the plan," stated

Below left: During renovation of Flood Park in the 1980s, workers made adobe bricks in essentially the same way they had been fashioned fifty years before.

Below right: Flood Park, a Depression-era creation, has been a popular South County recreation area since it was established.

19

Campbell. Tons of dirt, excavated by hand, were saved for making the adobe.

To the traditional recipe of dirt, clay, straw, and sand, Campbell added "bitumels," an asphalt-based waterproofing agent to give buildings greater longevity. After several unsuccessful attempts with the bread mixer, he achieved the desired adobe consistency and a more than satisfactory mixture was produced. In this manner, many thousands of adobe bricks were manufactured for use in constructing all the park buildings. "We made wood frames and scattered

The early park system was largely the creation of San Mateo County Parks Director Ralph Shaw, who headed the department from 1945 until 1971.

straw on the ground to keep the bricks from sticking to the soil. The frames were for two bricks, which was about all even a strong man could lift." The adobe mix was shoveled into the frames. "We then waited a couple of hours before taking frames off. The bricks were left in the sun for a week or so…and then we turned them over."

The caretaker's cottage, restrooms and administrative office building were constructed with the bricks. A small, one-room, single-story adobe structure required as many as 5,000 bricks. Redwood planks for the construction of benches, picnic tables and doors along with the roofing shingles were cut by WPA work teams at Memorial Park. All beams were hand hewn.

Ultimately the excavation became the swimming pool where thousands of county youngsters learned to swim. There were as many as 60,000 admissions each summer.

Especially during the 1940s and 1950s, when traveling by county residents was minimal, Flood Park became among the most popular relaxation and recreation spots in south San Mateo County. Bankers and janitors alike, just about everybody picnicked or played there. For company picnics, Flood Park was much in demand.

Ralph Howard Shaw, "Red," as he was known to those who worked with him early in his career, born in 1911, hailed

SAN MATEO COUNTY PARKS & RECREATION DIVISION

20

from Ritzville, Washington. He lived there until his family moved to California when Red was six.

Of Scots, English, and Dutch ancestry, he was a self-taught landscape artist who rounded out his education in recreation and park management with extension courses from the University of California. Shaw (1911-1997) landed his first job in recreation in 1940, as director, with the City of San Carlos.

Shaw, his wife Rey, and their one daughter lived at 927 Woodland Avenue in San Carlos. "He absolutely loved parks and loved his job. He never considered what he did to be work," remembers Rey Shaw.

In 1945, he was hired by San Mateo County to serve as Recreation Director. The following year, his title was changed to Director of Parks and Recreation.

Before long he was known as a "rangers' boss." Retired Memorial County Park Ranger Gary Woodhams reports that Shaw often put on his work clothes, grabbed a shovel, and worked right along with everybody else. Woodhams remembers him as a "great and honest man" whose "door was always open." Shaw was an "emotional" man who cared about his employees and who sincerely cared about their families.

"He spent a lot of time in the field and maintained close relationships with all his rangers," says Bob Emert. Shaw recognized that ranger compensation was meager. With that in mind, he introduced housing for rangers, building quarters for them in most of the parks. At first, rangers lived rent-free in return for a few extra hours of work.

But, adds Emert, Shaw was equally popular with the politicians. "He wore a suit and tie at the right times and made all the right sounds." Perhaps accounting for his popularity, when needed, he never hesitated to wade into the mud and mush even with his good shoes on. "We had no master plan except the one that was in Ralph's head."

Nita Spangler, for fourteen years a member of the County Park and Recreation Commission and a longtime park booster, remarked that the stocky, athletic Shaw devoted "his whole heart and soul to parks and was passionately devoted to building the system." Emert agrees, adding that Shaw was a "pugnacious visionary," often a "bulldog" who, when he wanted something, would "bite and hang on…. He was hardheaded and stubborn."

Shaw and his assistant, Jack Brook, weren't always in agreement. They could get into some real shouting matches that became legendary in the office. But that's also where the arguments ended. They had honest differences but the in-house dissent almost never became known by the public or the Board of Supervisors.

Ranger-naturalist Robert Breen, hired by Shaw in 1969, remembers him as "gruff, aggressive, rough, and ready." Nevertheless, concludes Emert, "Shaw was effective as a bridge builder and compromiser."

When he was hired, there were only two units, Memorial and Flood, in the county system, and a total of six full-time and seven part-time employees. His department's total budget for the year 1945 was $71,701.12.

As director of parks, Shaw's reputation soared and spread. He was enterprising and clever. For a quarter-century in San Mateo County, he championed the park system and played a key role in park acquisition and development. Bob Emert notes that Shaw

RECREATION

Organized recreation, once a major part of the department's responsibilities, gradually was phased out during the 1960s and 1970s. Directors Ralph Shaw and Jack Brook both had backgrounds in recreation and were committed to it. However, as the county's population grew, individual municipalities accepted greater responsibilities for their own programs. "The days of countywide yo-yo and jump rope contests ended," reports emeritus park administrator Bob Emert, who recalls his days as a "yo-yo guru" when he had been a recreation director at San Carlos.

For half a century, Flood Park's pool was probably South San Mateo County's most utilized recreational facility. Hundreds learned swimming there.

SAN MATEO COUNTY PARKS & RECREATION DIVISION

Glen Smith was hired by the department in 1953. Former Ranger Hector Berglund describes Smith as a "big lovable football-player type." Ultimately Smith became Chief of Recreation. He was totally dedicated to the principles of organized recreation. "He was a real missionary for his field," reports Assistant Parks Superintendent David Moore.

Smith became especially well-known at Memorial Park where he ran campfire programs. "He was determined to assure that camp guests enjoyed themselves," reports Ranger Ron Weaver. "Glen Smith brought a neighborhood atmosphere to the park setting." He encouraged campers to put on skits and was very effective organizing kids to stage plays at the campfires."

With proper ceremony, several times a year, Smith inducted new members into his Polar Bear Club. That is, robust park patrons were encouraged to jump into the frigid water of Pescadero Creek. Submerged to their necks, participants were then required to remain long enough to eat an Eskimo Pie.

Smith was awarded an academic degree in recreation during the 1970s. He subsequently taught the subject at Skyline College in San Bruno. "A number of our rangers, me included, took the class," reports Moore.

Among the county's most popular recreational activities was the swimming pool at Flood Park. The 180,000-gallon, unheated, sixty-by one-hundred-foot pool built in the 1930s, became the venue for regular swim meets. Ranger Ray Sycylo, who joined the department in 1958 and served twenty-eight years, was in charge. "We had a seven-person lifesaving crew. On warm days the pool really got crowded…. There could be up to 200 splashing about at any one time. Both swimming and canoeing classes were conducted in the pool. The long-antiquated pool was removed in the 1970s.

Flood Park's baseball diamond got almost constant use. Menlo-Atherton High School teams used it for practice. Semi-pro and college teams clashed there on weekends. "We would have great crowds in the stands," reports Sycylo.

Senior citizen enterprises, once largely confined to cards and bingo, became increasingly sophisticated and fell into the purview of recreation. Smith established the still-existent Senior Forum, a monthly countywide convocation that attracts representatives from each of the different communities.

Organized recreation halted abruptly in 1978 after funding cutbacks brought about by Proposition 13. Smith's position was abolished. Most aspects of that program have never been restored.

often found himself at odds with pure conservationists who felt that the forests should exclusively be preserved. "Ralph firmly believed that parks should be both used and preserved."

Much of his effort went into developing hiking and riding trails. He continued the earlier county policy of "land banking." Believing that the value of property was rising and would continue to do so, his thrust was to buy land, especially along the coast, where it could still be gotten relatively cheaply. He managed to acquire hundreds of acres for as little as five cents per acre.

In 1960, Shaw declined an offer to become the director of the California State Park and Recreation system. "He liked this county and loved the parks," says Rey Shaw, "San Mateo was the place for him."

When Shaw retired in 1971, his dynamic leadership was universally applauded. The San Mateo County park program was lauded by federal park officials who described it as "the most up-to-date in California and one of the best in the nation." Shaw headed a department of seventy-two permanent employees and twenty-eight seasonal workers in addition to sixty prison trustees and relief workers. His final budget was $2.6 million.

If Ralph Shaw was the giant behind the development of the San Mateo County Parks Department, landscape

Parks Planner Harry Dean (bearded and in his characteristic white hat) conducted a tour for supervisors in 1981. In the foreground is Supervisor William Schumaker.

architect Harry Dean Jr., a well-respected parks veteran, was the creative genius who brought the department up to a professional level and made the whole thing work. Perhaps no man left a more indelible imprint on the system. "He was the conscience of the department as long as he was here," states veteran ranger Tom Baker.

Dean was no neophyte to parks when he came to the county in 1971. Born in Long Island, New York, he received a degree from Syracuse University. "I started out to be a forester," he stated shortly before his retirement at age seventy, "then I shifted to landscape and recreation management, and finally ended up getting my degree in landscape architecture."

The former Marine Corps officer, who had fought in World War II and participated in planning for the invasion of Japan, came to California in 1950 to work for the National Park Service in Yosemite Valley as a planner. Thereafter, for sixteen years, he was employed by the California Division of Architecture.

In 1971, Dean talked with Ralph Shaw and was subsequently hired by San Mateo County as a landscape architect. "I was the first one employed by the county and thus gradually developed my own job description," he admitted. "And barely had I been hired than Shaw retired."

"Harry Dean was a marvel," states Olive Mayer of the Sierra Club and a leader in the early days of environmentalism. "He had a dream and followed it." During his twenty years with the county, Dean had a hand in improving every one of the county parks, historical sites, and trail systems.

"He was the key guy," adds County Ranger Michael W. Fritz. "Those were the important years. Dean worked under three directors — Shaw, Doc Mattison, and David Christy. "You always knew where you stood with Dean. He treated subordinates with respect and was good people." He was "dedicated" and "focused" and never hesitated to let his ideas be known. "He would bump heads, even with the directors," concludes Fritz. Dean and parks chief David Christy locked horns with regularity. "And," concludes David Moore, "Harry usually got his way."

"After a while, Coyote Point was my favorite park," Dean once confided. It was the first project that he tackled and he was responsible for laying out all the trails and meadow areas. "When I came to the county, the Point was just a small beach and a few picnic areas…the park had to be designed around the already existent rifle range, the museum and the marina."

What became the park was littered with debris and had become "a virtual garbage dump." By the time of Dean's retirement in 1991, Coyote Point Marina was recognized as one of the best on the bay and the only one that paid for itself. Furthermore, the park was the single most utilized unit in the system.

During his tenure as the landscape architect, four new parks were added: Edgewood in Redwood City, San Bruno Mountain State and County Park near Brisbane, San Pedro Valley in Pacifica, and portions of Pescadero Creek Park between La Honda and Pescadero.

The white-bearded Dean — no one remembers ever having seen him in a coat and tie — became acclaimed as a master trails man. "He brought consistency to trail standards," states Fritz who worked closely with the architect. During his career, Dean laid out hundreds of miles of trails, almost sixty miles of them in Pescadero Creek Park alone.

Commenting further about Dean, David Christy added: "In rain or shine, he could be found on hands and knees crawling through heavy brush placing flags to mark new hiking and riding trail routes." Under Dean's direction, trails were installed with consistent grades, never over ten percent. Gradually, where possible, the steepness was decreased to as little as five percent.

Perhaps no man in the parks department was ever more popular. His birthdays weren't celebrated because "he didn't believe in them." While rangers came to recognize him as "gentle and kind," they also saw Dean as tough.

"He'd come out with trail builder Gene Sheehan and we'd go out and flag the trails," reports Tom Baker. Ron Weaver, supervising ranger at San Bruno Mountain Park, recalls the rugged job of establishing trails through the thick and vicious coastal chaparral on the mountain. "Heavy brush and forests of poison oak didn't deter Harry at all."

SVANEVIK & BURGETT COLLECTION

In the laying out of San Pedro Valley Park, trails were cut through the dense coastal scrub. "We established the Hazelnut Trail with chain saws," states Jesse Gilley, "and our uniforms became black from the heavy oil of the poison oak."

"Unlike Shaw, Harry put everything on paper," states Bob Emert. "He really understood park planning and, once he did it, *nobody* interfered with his design."

Tree planting at Coyote Point was undertaken by horticultural wizard John McLaren in the 1880s. This view shows buildings of the Merchant Marine Academy and the early construction of the Coyote Point Marina.

Right: By 1900, Coyote Point, complete with bathhouse, had become a popular bathing beach for residents of Burlingame and San Mateo.

Below: Groups of young people, often seeking solitude where alcoholic beverages might be consumed away from public scrutiny, frequently made Coyote Point their destination.

BATH HOUSE AND BEACH, SAN MATEO, CAL.

Apparently there was at least one major difficulty with the county's long-term policy of land banking: unused land had a tendency to take on a life of its own and could easily get away.

Throughout the 1930s, park officials, with a dream of creating a large multi-purpose regional park in an area of high population density had jealously coveted Coyote Point in San Mateo. They found it a place of unusual beauty and began

gradually purchasing plots of land adjacent to the bay.

Coyote Point was originally an eighty-foot-high rocky knoll forming an island connected to the mainland by a marsh, which was subsequently drained and filled to create pasture land. In the nineteenth century, it was part of *Rancho San Mateo* owned by William Davis Merry Howard and his descendants. The land has had a checkered history.

Ample evidence has been found to indicate that this area was once inhabited by Native Californians who used it as a fishing area. Five shell middens and at least one prehistoric human burial have been unearthed. In 1987, while dredging was proceeding for the Coyote Point Yacht Harbor, an intact human skeleton was found in the mud, twelve feet below sea level. These skeletal remains were radiocarbon dated; results indicated that they were approximately 4,000 years old. Scholars presume that other prehistoric remains probably exist in the area.

In the years after 1860, several hundred Chinese squatters developed a thriving fishing village near the rocky point, primarily concentrating on harvesting bay shrimp for sale to San Francisco restaurants.

About the same time, owner George Howard, who acquired control of the land on the death of his brother, ordered construction of a road to the Point, and a wharf was built. The wharf, in operation by 1868, was used for the

landing of freight that was brought down the bay by barge or ship. Sometime later, this wharf was extended further out into the bay and rented to the Wisnom Lumber Company.[3]

Coyote Point pier provided valuable service during the period between 1888 and 1890, when the Spring Valley Water Company was constructing the huge concrete dam west of San Mateo across the neck of Crystal Springs Canyon. Cement for the project was brought from England to San Francisco and sent to San Mateo by rail, and sand, to be mixed with the cement, was brought by ship from the beaches of San Francisco.

For years, three schooners, loaded with Pacific sand, shuttled continually between North Beach and Coyote Point Wharf. A dozen six-horse teams, each dragging double wagons, moved throughout daylight hours from Coyote Point to San Mateo and thence up tortuous, winding, unpaved Crystal Spring Road to the construction site. In the process, teamsters ensured a daily sand delivery of 100 cubic yards. Ultimately, almost a million barrels were unloaded at Coyote Point Pier.

Earlier, between 1880 and 1882, Scotsman John McLaren, a horticultural specialist who had been trained at the Royal Botanical Gardens in Edinburgh, was brought to the United States by the Howard family. Possessing a great

---

[3]*William Davis Merry Howard, a pioneer San Francisco merchant, married Agnes Poett in 1849. He died in 1856. His widow married the deceased man's brother George. George Howard died in 1879. Agnes Poett Howard then remarried, this time to Burlingame attorney Henry Pike Bowie. During the 1880s and the 1890s, Coyote Point was owned by the Bowie Estate Company; a portion of the property was under the ownership of William Henry Howard, son of the original owner.*

This photograph of Coyote Point shows the precise location of Pacific City, the 1920s amusement park. It clearly points out the sophistication of the operation.

fascination for fast-growing eucalyptus — Australian gum trees — McLaren directed the planting of the bald point with these tall-growing trees. A forest, initially of approximately 70,000 seedlings, was planted. Today, although many of the trees have been removed and others have died, Coyote Point Park is still characterized by a eucalyptus forest.

By the 1890s, the adjacent sandy bathing beach had become the San Mateo and Burlingame area's most celebrated recreational attraction. It was known for its

CONEY ISLAND OF THE WEST

Investors in Pacific City thrilled at the size of initial crowds. But many factors combined to bring about the early failure of the enterprise.

Pacific City opened in San Mateo at the foot of Peninsula Avenue July 1, 1922. On Independence Day, 100,000 people went through the turnstiles.

Pacific City was a paradise for youngsters. Four acres were set aside exclusively as playground. Topping the list of wonderful attractions was the roller coaster, the second largest in the United States and unquestionably the fastest in the West. More than one youngster was scared out of years of growth by its near-vertical dive of eighty feet.

Food concessionaires did brisk business in waffles, ice cream, hot dogs, and popcorn. The *Ocean Wave*, an old ferryboat steamer, in addition to having been a one-time Merchant Marine training ship during World War I, was tied up to the new 500-foot-long pier and transformed into a semi-elegant floating cafeteria and grill for 750 diners.

Crowds delighted at finding an elaborate dance pavilion fronting on the boardwalk, large enough to accommodate 2,000 wildly gyrating couples. There was a bathhouse with 1,000 changing rooms. On sunny days, thousands frolicked in the bay.

There was always something going on — baseball games, track meets, and sporting events of all varieties. Special days for kids featured baby buggy parades, gingham gown revues, and Punch & Judy shows. Big, in summer of 1922, was the Hawaiian Carnival featuring Island singers, hula dancers, and surfboarders. A top draw was a young escape artist by the name of Houdini who challenged local policemen to test their skills at keeping him locked up. None succeeded.

Private parties at Pacific City became all the rage. Local youngsters held birthday celebrations there. In August 1922, an international association of 2,000 fire chiefs and 70,000 members of the Woodsmen of the World swept in. The Columbus Day gala, staged by the Knights of Columbus, was transformed into an amazing extravaganza. Seventy-five thousand showed up to watch 1,000 actors restage the landing of Columbus in the New World.

shallow, warm water that often reached a comfortable seventy degrees in summertime. A bathhouse was constructed there and used continually until the early 1920s.

Coyote Point became so popular that it was highlighted in travel magazines. "There is no pleasanter spot on the bay for an outing than the 'Coyote.' There is good bathing, fishing, boating and clam-digging, and the clean sandy beach is a positive joy for children." Hunters also gravitated to the area where the supply of game birds seemed unlimited.

A eucalyptus-lined walking trail led from Burlingame to the beach. Coyote Point became a popular destination for cyclists, especially after 1890 when bicycles became an increasingly fashionable form of recreation.

During the 1890s, the beach became threatened with ruination by repeated visits of "sand pirates." For years, intent on gathering sand for sale to artificial stone manufacturers in San Francisco, these pirates carried away fifty to a hundred tons per load. Large portions of the beach, soon characterized by rock and mud, were rendered useless.[4]

During and immediately following World War I, the U.S. Navy briefly considered making Coyote Point, which the government felt to be well protected from potential invaders entering the Golden Gate, the headquarters of the Pacific Fleet. This idea was soon abandoned.

Instead, July 1, 1922, Pacific City, a grand amusement park backed by local chambers of commerce as a way to attract people to the county, opened at Coyote Point. It was

---

[4]*Because of this long-term damage to the beach, in 1967, the county trucked in 10,000 tons of sand scraped from the Great Highway in San Francisco following sandstorms.*

touted as the "greatest fun community since the creation of Coney Island" and the "most marvelous bathing beach on the Pacific Coast." Boosters predicted that the enterprise would rival the great resorts of Southern California. Pacific City was centered on a 3,200-foot boardwalk stretching along a mile of sandy beach. Few visitors, who marveled at the soft, white sand, realized that 2,000 tons had been trucked in from the beaches of Monterey.

Pacific City proved to be an ill-fated endeavor. In spite of an attendance of approximately 1,000,000 during its first year, the much ballyhooed enterprise didn't manage to survive a second season. A fire destroyed part of the complex. Especially cool weather in 1923, accompanied by a foul stench caused by Burlingame's sewer system, which emptied into the bay, contributed to the premature bankruptcy of the enterprise.

After eyeing this valuable property for several decades and fully realizing its potential, in 1940, San Mateo County Park and Recreation Department purchased 727 acres at Coyote Point. About half the acreage, 329 acres, was beneath the shallows of the bay. The purchase included 7,000 feet of shoreline. Typically, except for the beach used by swimmers and sun worshipers, park development was not immediately undertaken.

MERCHANT MARINE TRAINING AT COYOTE POINT

During World War II, officers at the U.S. Merchant Marine Academy supervised "abandon ship" drills from the Coyote Point pier.

At Coyote Point, there was a cadre of fifty-three Navy and Merchant Marine officers along with 150 enlisted personnel.

Cadet-midshipmen studying to be deck officers found the curriculum concentrated on principles of navigation, mathematics, charts, and nautical astronomy. There was instruction in signaling with a blinker, semaphore, and international code flags. Instructors taught rope handling, use of winches, and techniques of loading and unloading a ship amid adverse conditions.

Those working to qualify as engineering officers labored below decks learning to fire boilers and maintain engines. Concentration was on both steam and diesel engineering, electricity, and fire control.

In addition to Navy Science (taught by a commissioned officer), men in both divisions studied ordnance and gunnery. For this training, cadets were bussed over the mountain to Point Montara near Moss Beach. Men were also trained in the use of small arms.

Physical training was vigorous and demanding. Men climbed ropes and cargo nets. They practiced crawling through portholes and swimming submerged in dark, oily, and sometimes burning water. At the end of the long pier, a double-decked tower, the height of a three-story building had been erected. Cadets were required to climb to the top and dive into the bay. This exercise was essential because of the frequency with which Merchant mariners were required to leap from sinking ships into turbulent ocean waters. Men who could not bring themselves to make the dive were "bilged" out of the program. Their records simply noted that they were "study casualties."

SAN MATEO COUNTY HISTORICAL ASSOCIATION

After the outbreak of World War II in Europe during September 1939, the United States was gradually but relentlessly pulled toward involvement. Nevertheless, because the prevailing national attitude was that Americans should carefully steer clear of this European struggle, the country did little to prepare. Thus, in December 1941, after the Japanese sank much of the Pacific Fleet in their attack on Pearl Harbor, Hawaii, the United States had much catching up to do.

Shipyards boomed. More than 282,000 shipbuilders were employed in California by August 1943. Industrialist Henry J. Kaiser, one of many contractors, was turning out a new freighter every ten hours.

Providing officers for these new vessels became one of the war's major undertakings. The U.S. Merchant Marine Academy at Kings Point, New York, proved incapable of turning out an adequate number of officers. The Maritime Commission, believing the knoll amid the trees to be an ideal site for training, eyed the unused land at Coyote Point. County supervisors received a request from the Commission and felt it would be in the public interest that the maritime school be established at Coyote Point. Ultimately, in spring of 1942, twenty-six acres were made available to the Maritime Commission for the remainder of the war.

On June 25, 1942, an army of 400 workers undertook another of the many miracles of World War II, blazing through a dense jungle of vicious poison oak and the thick eucalyptus entanglements of Coyote Point. Just sixty-five days later, classrooms, gymnasium, a machine shop,

SVANEVIK & BURGETT COLLECTION

infirmary, a dock, and fourteen redwood barracks for 336 cadet-midshipmen had been completed. Although site development continued for a year, the base was deemed ready for occupancy.

The school at San Mateo Point, as the Navy called the facility, offered accelerated courses for deck and engineering officers. This was the largest of two such training centers in the nation. (The other was at Pass Christian, Mississippi.) The mission at Coyote Point was to offer the *basic* course for third mates or third assistant engineering officers in just ninety days. Thereafter, following six months of sea duty, the

For years this globe and anchor were symbols of the U.S. Merchant Marine Academy at Coyote Point. After the school closed, they remained behind as a memorial to Merchant Mariners who had been killed during the war.

31

COLLEGE OF SAN MATEO

Much to the dissatisfaction of the Parks and Recreation Department, after the war, the former U.S. Merchant Marine Academy was turned over to San Mateo Junior College. Planners had hoped to transform it into a major recreation area.

full twenty-two-month course was completed at Kings Point. This was considered equivalent to a pre-war, four-year program of study.

Steamship companies clamored for Coyote Point graduate officers. By June 1944, 4,111 had successfully completed the course. The school briefly survived the end of the war in 1945. But in January 1947, budget cuts forced closure of the San Mateo Point facility.

Nevertheless, a poignant memorial to Coyote Point graduates still is a highlight of the county park. A granite plaque, mounted at a site overlooking the bay, reads: "This memorial is dedicated to the memory of the cadet-midshipmen and graduates of the United States Merchant Marine Cadet Corps who gave the last full measures of devotion for our country during World War II, 1941-1945."

At the war's end, Ralph Shaw and the San Mateo County Parks Commission, noting the desperate need for recreational facilities — indeed the county population had grown by 110 percent since 1940 — expected that Coyote Point should and would be returned to the county for the development of a park.

But park people were again destined for bitter disappointment. San Mateo Junior College, established in 1922, had never had a genuine campus of its own. Within three decades, the college had moved between the old San Mateo High School building on Baldwin Avenue to a dilapidated mansion in San Mateo's Central Park. During the 1930s, construction had been begun on a new, albeit never completed, campus at Delaware and Peninsula avenues.

College officials, in 1947, surveyed Coyote Point as a potential site for a new campus to accommodate the thousands of students expected to enroll in the aftermath of the war under the auspices of the G.I. Bill of Rights. The college's president, Charles S. "Jumbo" Morris, believed that the then vacant Merchant Marine buildings, though battered, were ready for occupancy and would be an ideal setting for the school.

Disgruntled park officials argued that whereas a college campus at Coyote Point would serve several thousand students annually, more than a million people a year could be expected to use the land if it were placed in the hands of the Parks Department. Furthermore, Ralph Shaw pointed out, there were no other suitable sites for a much-needed regional park development in that section of the county.

It was finally agreed that San Mateo Junior College would be allowed to locate at Coyote Point "for a year or two." The agreement stipulated that when enrollments, grossly expanded by veterans returning from overseas leveled off, the San Mateo County Parks and Recreation Department would again be allowed to take possession of the property.

College classes at Coyote Point began in 1947. Merchant Marine buildings, designed from the start to have been temporary and now well-worn by wartime use, proved from the start to be inadequate for academic purposes. The one-time Merchant Marine chapel was transformed into the college library. Old Matson Hall became the cafeteria. The campus was directly under the landing pattern of San Francisco Airport. Planes overhead constantly rattled windows and buildings.

Though conscientious educators pointed out these shortcomings and what they continually described as "nightmarish" teaching conditions, county voters were disinclined to approve necessary funds for construction of a new college campus. Thus, what was supposed to have been merely a temporary expedient became at least semi-permanent. Coyote Point remained San Mateo Junior College's primary campus until 1963.[5]

Driving the road from the highway into Coyote Point was a unique experience that few students ever forgot. The road was narrow, winding, and riddled with deep crevices and erosion scars. Unpaved parking lots, pitted with deep holes, became an ongoing joke. Students spoke seriously about cars that "went down last winter and weren't found until June."

The Commandant's House, former residence of the Maritime Academy's commanding officer, a one-story, relatively modern structure, was set among a picturesque grove of eucalyptus trees. The dwelling, along with its spacious sheltered patio, was used for meetings of college trustees, faculty, and students.

Unlike most educators, Elon Hildreth, who replaced Morris as president of San Mateo Junior College in 1952, was totally enamored with Coyote Point's tranquil setting. The site, among the eucalyptus trees on the edge of the bay, fit his concept of where a college should be placed. He began a campaign to make Coyote Point the site of a new permanent

---

[5]*San Mateo Junior College was established in 1922. At that time, it was regarded as an institution that provided the first two years of a university education. However, by the 1930s, it was gradually transforming into a community college, offering courses both to potential university scholars and to others involved in vocational pursuits — fire science, horticulture, nursing and cosmetology — to name a few. By 1953, both faculty and students agreed that the word "junior" should be dropped from the name of the college. After much consideration, the name College of San Mateo was adopted and approved by the college trustees in April 1954.*

COYOTE POINT MUSEUM FOR ENVIRONMENTAL EDUCATION

The famed Coyote Point Museum for Environmental Education began in a surplus World War II Quonset hut as the San Mateo County Junior Museum during the 1950s.

For fourteen years, the Junior Museum operated as a private institution. However, in 1967, after protracted study, the museum was incorporated into the San Mateo County Parks and Recreation Department's new Interpretive Division. Parks and Recreation assumed the responsibility for operating the popular facility. Maryanne Danielson served as the museum director.

From the beginning, operating funds were raised by the Coyote Point Museum Auxiliary, a hardworking cadre of women volunteers who established the non-profit organization in 1953. After experimenting with numerous innovative fund-raising techniques, in 1958, the Auxiliary tested a unique new idea, the so-called Decorators' Show

SAN MATEO COUNTY PARKS & RECREATION DIVISION

House. They planned to open one of Hillsborough's great houses. Each room was to be decorated by a different interior designer. The Show House became an overnight success and a virtual Peninsula institution. The lure of lavish houses combined with venerable old family names attracted thousands from all over California.

The museum acquired a new name and scope in March 1973. Thereafter, it became the Coyote Point Museum for Environmental Education. The goal was for the museum to become a learning place for all ages — "a place where extraordinary ways of looking at the ordinary would make each visitor responsive to San Mateo County's precious heritage of ocean and bay, of grasslands and mountains…." All revolved around a planned new resource center. The new facility, crowning the crest of a eucalyptus-covered hill, began to rise at Coyote Point Park.

In 1978, following the passage of California's Proposition 13, a measure limiting property taxes, the Parks Department was faced with severe budget reductions. The Parks Interpretive Division was abolished. Shortly thereafter, museum control passed from operation by the county back to the Coyote Point Museum Association.

An elaborate $1.9 million, 28,000-square-foot Coyote Point Museum for Environmental Education, paid for by the county, officially opened to the public May 16, 1981.

The privately paid staff was headed by museum director Linda Liebes.[6]

The museum opening marked the culmination of years of fund-raising and planning by the Coyote Point Museum Auxiliary. The museum is characterized by a spacious four-level exhibition hall and animal center. Those who normally thought of museums as dreary and dark found this new institution a warm refreshing treat.

Visitors listen to the actual sounds of rattlesnakes, smell skunks and have the opportunity to watch bees building a hive.

Today the museum is run by the Coyote Point Museum Association. The grounds are maintained by the San Mateo County Park and Recreation Department.

---

[6]Linda Liebes was one of the original planners of the Coyote Point Museum for Environmental Education. She began working with Coyote Point Museum when it was a county-run, outdoor animal park for children. She worked to raise money for the new museum and was named director in 1975. Construction was completed in 1981. The elegant building houses the Environmental Hall, an 8,000-square-foot room with sculptures, computer games, live insects and a salt-water aquarium, which explains the ecosystem of the Bay Area. An outdoor exhibit of native plants and animals wasn't completed until 1991. Liebes had a passion for the environment and, during her tenure as director, successfully conveyed that passion to visitors. She stepped down from her position in 1996.

campus. As if to legitimize this effort, Hildreth and his wife moved into the Commandant's House, thereafter referring to it as the "President's Home." It became the site of faculty luncheons and receptions, fashion shows, and holiday teas.[7]

Hildreth's attitude, plans, and action caused tremendous animosity between the college and many San Mateo County officials who felt that the new president had broken a "gentlemen's agreement," that is, the understanding that after the post-war boom, the college would return Coyote Point to the county for use as a public recreational area.[8]

The battle for Coyote Point, involving the college and the Parks and Recreation Commission spurred on by Ralph Shaw, became increasingly vicious. Both sides lobbied in Washington. There was a barrage of correspondence and ultimately an investigation by the San Mateo County Grand Jury.

---

[7]This structure, currently known as the "Captain's House," has served a variety of purposes. Not only was it the commandant's quarters during the Merchant Marine years and, for a time the president's house during the era of the college. Later it doubled as the home for San Mateo County Parks and Recreation Chief Kermit Vangene and, in 1970, the office of San Mateo County Supervisor Robert St. Clair. Currently it is used as a training facility for the county and may also be rented by private groups for special seminars.

[8]Hildreth was unsuccessful in his effort to permanently acquire Coyote Point as a new campus. Amid increased opposition to a number of his policies, he resigned as president of the college in 1955. Subsequently he was employed by the U.S. Department of State. Hildreth was sent to Saigon, Vietnam, to assist in reorganizing the South Vietnamese schools and, in the process, help ensure the "continuing health of that nation's democratic tradition."

A dredge beginning the creation of a basin for the Coyote Point Marina.

SAN MATEO COUNTY PARKS & RECREATION DIVISION

During the college years, development of other sections of Coyote Point still under county ownership was undertaken. Articles of incorporation for a junior museum had been signed at Coyote Point in April 1953. The following year a surplus Quonset hut, on college property opened as the newly-created San Mateo County Junior Museum. This free facility was jointly sponsored by the San Francisco Junior League and the National Foundation for Junior Museums. The institution was designed to benefit the children and youth of the county by introducing them to the wonderland of nature.

Live domestic animals, including hamsters, rabbits, and white rats, along with full directions for their care and feeding, were lent to school classes for short periods. The museum also provided such animals to individual children to be taken home for brief periods of study and care.

Meanwhile the Parks and Recreation Commission never abandoned the dream of a regional park at Coyote Point. The general plan was to encompass the whole area and, if necessary, include the college campus as well. Thus, during the college era, Parks Director Shaw planned and undertook a series of developmental measures.

Earlier yachting activity had been primarily centered off the old Pacific City beach. The only facilities comprised eucalyptus logs for floats and rickety eucalyptus piers held together with whatever happened to be available.

Dredging was begun for an elaborate new harbor, which Shaw ultimately hoped would accommodate 1,000 boats. On a number of occasions throughout the years, these plans were modified. By 2000, there were two basins and only 565 berths. Piles of broken concrete, salvaged after the wrecking of the old San Mateo - Hayward Bridge, are piled nearby for use in the projected construction of a third basin.

Not far from the beach, in 1961, workers began excavating a quarry for construction of the Coyote Point Rifle and Pistol Range, an $80,000 project. The facility was one of the first National Rifle Association-approved safety ranges to be constructed in the United States. Not long after opening in 1962, it was rated as one of the finest ranges on the Pacific Coast. Initially, access was open to all county residents. In recent years, however, its use has been more restrictive. Safety of the facility had been questioned after at least one person claimed to have been injured by a wild shot and several reported that bullets had narrowly missed them. Unquestionably, trees in the park have become peppered with bullet holes. Presently supervised by the County Sheriff, the range is maintained under especially tight management and limited to use solely by law enforcement agencies.

The swimming beach was improved and a parking area and bathhouse were not constructed until the 1970s. A picnic ground was also added. The problem of disappearing sand was solved through the introduction of pea-gravel. (Regulations presently forbid the introduction of any new gravel or sand. Rangers, however, note that while the beach diminishes in winter, sand returns each spring.)

Throughout most of the twentieth century, shelter from northwest winds offered by Coyote Point has provided a popular anchorage for pleasure boats bound for San Mateo. The Coyote Point Yacht Club, a private organization which leases land from the county, was incorporated in 1941. Its first clubhouse, a modest single-story structure, was completed two years later. A much more elaborate, spacious, 7,000-square-foot, two-deck yachting headquarters, which stands atop pilings driven sixty-five feet onto the floor of the bay, opened in March 1968. This nautically-flavored clubhouse, the pride of its members, has a dining room large enough to seat 300.

Coyote Point Yacht Club achieved a degree of notoriety in June 1947, through its sponsorship of the First Annual Shark Derby, the only shark-fishing competition in the United States at that time. Derbies were held at Coyote Point from 1947-1952. In 1947, 1,000 attended to watch the efforts of 360 participants. A total of 104 sharks were hooked. Barbara Alexander of Burlingame took the top award by landing a fifty-eight-inch, thirty-pound mud shark. By 1949, 20,000 spectators were in attendance.

President Harry Truman added luster to the second Shark Derby in 1948 when he agreed to order a fifteen-minute train stop in Burlingame on the night of June 13. Almost 10,000 Peninsulans turned out to greet the feisty president at the Burlingame Railroad Depot. Truman, on the observation car of the Presidential Special, was given a set of fishing tackle by Commodore Andy Byrd of the Coyote Point Yacht Club. Obviously pleased with the memento, Truman whipped the pole over the heads of the crowd.

Members also presented the president with a "Kingfisher Derby." Apparently grateful, although somewhat less enthusiastic, Truman laughingly regarded the elegant, conspicuously labeled hat with Missouri suspicion. He held the derby in his hands but, despite urging, bashfully refused to model it for the gathered throng. A Boy Scout band played for the occasion.

A week later, when the Shark Derby was staged, a total of 364 sharks were hooked. The biggest, a thirty-six pounder, was taken by Jack Miller of Burlingame. A salmon barbecue finished off the day.

Above: President Harry S Truman stopped in Burlingame (1948) to highlight the Coyote Point Shark Derby.

Below: Coyote Point's Marina became one of the most popular berthing spots on the bay.

A Japan Air Lines DC-8, flopped into the bay short of the airport in 1968. What could have been a major disaster ended well.

Rescued passengers from the Japan Air Lines jet that slammed into the bay were pulled to safety at the Coyote Point Marina.

CRASH OF JAPAN AIR LINES DC-8

It was Friday morning, November 22, 1968, when Japan Air Lines Flight 2 from Tokyo to New York via Honolulu and San Francisco, with ninety-six passengers and eleven crewmen aboard belly-flopped into the bay while making its approach to San Francisco International Airport. The giant DC-8, bearing the name *Shiga*, which came down three miles short of the runway, was a quarter-mile from the Coyote Point Yacht Club.

Though the pilot radioed that all aboard were safe, government and airport officials were disbelieving. Newsmen converged on Coyote Point. The huge plane, with its nose turned toward the Yacht Club, was clearly visible through very thick fog. Resting on the mud in seven feet of water, the plane appeared like a giant sea bird or sitting duck.

There was no panic aboard the airliner. Five large yellow life rafts were inflated and loaded. These were dragged by rescue boats to the boat ramp at Coyote Point Yacht Club. While most barefooted passengers appeared shaken, they seemed to have taken the splashdown in stride. The majority impatiently bypassed a coffee bar set up for them at the Yacht Club.

John Marchi, chief of the South San Francisco Fire Department, was one of the first officials on the scene. He declared that the crash was a "one in a million shot." Had the plane come down in shallower water there almost certainly would have been a smashup and fire. Had the water been any deeper, the big plane would have "sunk like a rock." Amazed airport officials later declared that the Coyote Point Reef was the only place in the entire bay where such a landing could have ever been effected.

Until that time, this was history's single most successful ditching of a jet airliner.

Coyote Point Harbor Master Arthur O'Leary and members of his staff, who, in the harbor's twenty-six-foot skiff, were the first to reach the stricken craft, received commendations from the San Mateo County Board of Supervisors for their work in rescuing passengers. The park skiff pulled the first two rafts of passengers ashore.

County parks director Shaw took advantage of this dramatic occasion to warn of potential dangers at Coyote Point. He noted that the harbor staff were called upon eighty to 100 times per year to make rescues. The successful rescue resulted in the acquisition of a new patrol boat for Coyote Point Marina.

Elon Hildreth resigned as president of the College of San Mateo in 1956. He was replaced by Julio Bortolazzo, the son of Italian-American immigrant parents. This dynamic educator-politician, with a doctorate from Harvard, succeeded with the college where others before him had failed. Soon after Bortolazzo's arrival, San Mateo County voters approved a multi-million dollar bond issue for the construction of a new campus at College Heights, in the hills west of San Mateo. Classes opened at the new state-of-the-art facility in September 1963.

Shortly thereafter, the college at long last vacated Coyote Point. At that time, the property was sold to the county, which realized its long-term dream of acquiring the Point exclusively for park purposes. A master plan for the development of picnic and recreation areas was created in March 1963.

Since the 1970s, Coyote Point, visited by more than half a million people annually, has become the most popular and most utilized park in the county system.

Supervising Ranger Jesse Gilley, with the parks department for thirty years and intermittently associated with Coyote Point from the beginning, notes that even the brisk afternoon winds, which blow almost consistently from May through September, don't deter those who have come to love the park.

It is exceedingly popular for kite flying. Approximately 450 windsurfers use the park on a regular basis. On good days, scores take to the swells. Hobicat and swimming races are regularly scheduled there as well.

Outdoor weddings beneath the eucalyptus have become popular.

During the decade after World War II, the population of the county doubled and there was much greater emphasis on recreational activities for its residents. Two important historical properties were acquired by the parks department, Woodside Store and the Sanchez Adobe.

The first of the county-owned properties was Woodside Store, a small, unpainted, and apparently insignificant structure made of redwood cut from the nearby forest. It is located in the forest at the intersection of Kings Mountain and Tripp roads.

For a time, this store was the only one on the Peninsula between San Francisco and Santa Clara. It was a mere shack built by partners Mathias Parkhurst and Robert Orville Tripp in 1851. That original structure was destroyed by fire and the present larger building was erected in May 1854.

Barn-like and unsophisticated in design, Woodside Store, with a double-gabled roof and wide veranda, became the thriving heart of business and cultural activities for the logging community. During the 1850s, Peninsula logging prospered when local lumber was much in demand for construction of Gold Rush San Francisco, fifteen water-powered and steam-powered sawmills were operating within a five-mile radius of the store's front porch. More than a thousand lumberjacks were harvesting lumber and shingles from the primeval forest.

Woodside Store was noteworthy; it was more than a general merchandizing emporium. The store housed the only U.S. Post Office in the redwoods and also served as a bank.

Woodside Family Groceries as it appeared during the 1890s.

SAN MATEO COUNTY PARKS & RECREATION DIVISION

At least for a time, the building contained the only safe on the Peninsula. Upon the death of Parkhurst in 1863, Robert Orville Tripp became the store's sole proprietor.

"Doc," as the tall, thin, pipe-smoking, and ever-popular, Tripp was commonly known, had been trained in Philadelphia as a dentist. Upon reaching the redwoods, he set up a dental chair in a corner of the store and routinely plugged or pulled teeth for lumberjacks in pain. In San Francisco, the price of an extraction was an ounce of gold or $16. Doc Tripp was more than willing to yank a diseased tooth for as little as $4.

Early store advertisements offered clothes, liquors, wines, hardware supplies, food, fancy goods, tobacco products and agricultural implements. All were offered at "reasonable prices." There were jars of licorice, rock candy, and shoofly crackers. Soda crackers sold for thirteen cents a pound during the 1850s. Coffee was twenty cents a pound.

No doctors were yet established on the Peninsula. Thus patent medicines were always big sellers at Woodside Store. A wide selection included Dr. Payne's Sanative Pills, flour, sulphur, Thomson's Eye Water, calciumed magnesia, gum camphor, and the ever-popular castor oil.

Woodside Store became the transportation hub of the redwood country. Regular stagecoach service from Redwood City to the store dated from 1852. A thrice-weekly schedule was initiated between San Francisco and the store in 1853. This was soon replaced by daily, six-hour transit in each direction. Stagecoaches on the regular trek from Redwood City to the coastal village of Pescadero were all routed via Woodside Store. The store never became the center of a town largely because its owner adamantly refused to sell any of the land around it.

While Tripp was a founder of the Mountain Dell Division No. 74, Sons of Temperance, an organization primarily of lumberjacks who met at the store, he had no compunctions about selling alcohol. Though there was much drinking in and about the store, it was never an official saloon. When paying their monthly bills, customers were offered a liquid libation in the proprietor's office. Tripp's dental customers were also given spirits to ease their pain. Teamsters who drove wagonloads of logs down Kings Mountain Road, frequently stopped by the store in search of a little something to steady their nerves.

Tripp, who built one of the Peninsula's first wineries, stocked quality spirits as well as cheaper barreled whiskey, which was ladled into whatever container that was brought in by a customer. Loggers often mixed whiskey with turpentine to make a fuel that they burned to heat coffee. Not surprisingly, Woodside Store became the favorite venue for local weekend jollifications.

Logging on the east side of the mountain ridge reached its peak by 1859. Thereafter, while logging continued west of the summit, the area around the store gradually evolved into a farming community. The Woodside Library Association was formed in 1858 by residents who paid a quarter per month for membership. The initial 190-book collection was briefly housed in the attic of Woodside Store.

Through long life, both store and proprietor acquired venerability. By the time of his death at age 93 in 1909, Tripp had become perhaps the greatest legend of the redwoods.

Recognizing the historical importance of the store, although it was then in a tilting and dilapidated condition, San Mateo County purchased it in 1940. Subsequently the structure was turned over to the Parks and Recreation Department.

During the 1980s, a major restoration project was undertaken to assure that Woodside Store would continue to stand and be appreciated by generations yet to come. Almost half a million dollars were poured into righting and restoring the sagging structure.

Today this store, the oldest wood frame construction in the county, is open to the public as a museum under the auspices of the San Mateo County Historical Association. It has been restored to the ambiance of the 1880s. Unquestionably, Woodside Store is a community treasure.

But of all the historical structures in San Mateo County, Sanchez Adobe, located along Linda Mar Boulevard in today's incorporated city of Pacifica, is one of the oldest and most exciting. Within its grounds lies evidence of every period in San Mateo County history. Certainly it is a strong link to the region's prehistoric and Hispanic past.

The tranquil site nestled in the fertile, picturesque and, once-upon-a-time grizzly bear-infested San Pedro Valley, was a campsite for coastal natives. It is

Store proprietor Robert Orville Tripp continued to operate his establishment until after the beginning of the twentieth century.

PREHISTORIC COASTAL DWELLERS

Archaeological excavations at the adobe site have revealed numerous clues about the existence of coastal dwellers who inhabited the area before the Spanish arrival.

If history is correctly defined as a written record, California's historic period began with the arrival of Spaniards in 1769.

Spanish missionaries estimated that perhaps 10,000 natives lived along the coast between Point Sur and San Francisco Bay. And they believed that the population of the Peninsula consisted of approximately 1,500 individuals. During the eighteenth century, Europeans commonly referred to these natives as *Costeños*, coastal dwellers. Over time, the word mutated, gradually becoming *Costanoan*.

This name was never used by local inhabitants who lived in small tribes, seldom larger than several hundred in number and each of which had its own unique name. There was no single tribe or nation.

Linguistic differences were great; most could not communicate with one another.

Spanish priests ordered construction of a mission outpost, *San Pedro y San Pablo*, on the site of *Pruristac*, a village in the San Pedro Valley. The native settlement was tiny, containing a mere handful of dwellings.

Simultaneously, the village of *Chagunte* was located in the area of present-day Princeton on the San Mateo coast; the village of *Ssatumnumo* was thought to have been in Half Moon Bay. The *Cotogenes* lived on Purisima Creek. Several hundred natives, calling themselves *Oljones*, lived near San Gregorio.

Twentieth-century descendants of *Costanoans* acquired tremendous disdain for the appellation, no doubt, in part, because it was a creation of Spanish conquerors. Even though the name *Oljones* was originally used to identify the natives of the San Gregorio area, many expressed a preference for that name, or as it became Americanized, *Ohlone*. Today, the word *Ohlone*, albeit incorrectly, is applied to all coastal native dwellers. It is equally as much a stereotype as the word *Costanoan*.

By whatever names they used or are presently known as, significant anthropological and archeological evidence of native Californians has been found in a number of areas that have become San Mateo County parks.

SAN MATEO COUNTY PARKS & RECREATION DIVISION

There is no greater treasure trove of native artifacts than those found in San Pedro Valley, notably on the property of the Sanchez Adobe. Not surprisingly, relics dating from the mission era have been found. However, significant evidence has surfaced indicating that the area was a native habitation millenniums before the arrival of the Spaniards.

Other parks are also rich in artifacts. Middens have been found at Junipero Serra Park in San Bruno. A number of native relics are displayed in the park office. Other middens have been preserved at the Fitzgerald Marine Reserve on the bluffs overlooking Moss Beach. A native burial ground has been pinpointed on the east slope of Mount San Bruno and will ultimately become part of the State and County Park. At least one native remain was unearthed in the mud during excavation for the Coyote Point Marina, indicating that there was an aboriginal presence at that area as well.

As a rule, native Californians found the redwoods to be dark and foreboding. They usually avoided the canyons of the Sierra Morena where the giant redwoods cast their eerie elongated shadows. Not only was the food supply beneath the redwood canopy restricted, some natives believed that these giant sentinels of the forest somehow contained the spirits of their ancestors.

approximately a mile inland from the beach, thus free of most coastal fogs. Prehistoric habitation has been confirmed through the recovery of numerous Native American artifacts. A number of skeletal remains were exhumed there by archaeologists in the 1950s. These bones were boxed and turned over to the anthropology department at Cañada College in Redwood City.

In 1998, Professor Gary Paul of San Francisco State University, while conducting an archaeology class on the site, located another partial skeletal remain. These bones were estimated to be approximately 500 years old. In that they were buried just a few feet from the surface and found in proximity of decorative bird whistles made of bone, the person, a young woman, is believed to have been one of significance. At least initially, attempts were made to keep this find a secret. However, after consultation with a local Native American organization that conducted an appropriate ceremony, the bones were reinterred on the grounds of the adobe in an unmarked grave.

On this same land, in the mid-1780s, Spanish Franciscan padres of *Mission San Francisco de Asís*, employing Indian labor, created an outpost called *San Pedro y San Pablo* (St. Peter and St. Paul) where farms and orchards were established to provide the mission with food. But less than a decade after its beginning, the *rancho* was visited by an epidemic that killed large numbers of the Native American population. Convinced that the region was cursed, many natives fled. Unable to stem the flight, the Spanish abandoned the site, moving the primary mission farm to what is today the town of San Mateo.

THE CALIFORNIOS

The people of Mexico, many of them full-blooded Spaniards, completed a successful revolution against imperial Spain in 1821. Thereafter, what had been New Spain became the State of Mexico with the northern provinces of Texas, New Mexico, and Alta California.

Mexico officially ruled California until the occupation by Americans in 1846. These few years constituted the most colorful and legendary epoch in California's history. As a generality, few Californians chose to refer to themselves as Mexicans. In fact, they adopted a new term, almost universally calling themselves *Californios*.

This was a storied era of beautiful men, handsome women, and magnificent horses. The population was small. Typically, men dressed in short jackets with embroidered velvet lapels, colorful silk sashes tied around their waists, and characteristic flat black felt hats lined with white silk. Horses were generally adorned with silver saddles and bridles.

The world of the *Californios* was a leisure society characterized by gaming, horse racing, and dancing by those of European descent. *Californios* were celebrated both for their large families and their hospitality that apparently knew no bounds. All work, in an economic environment not unlike that found in the American South during the antebellum period, was performed by California's native population.

Francisco Sanchez (1805-1862), the eldest son of José Antonio Sanchez, was one of ten children. He also became the father of ten.

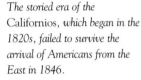

The storied era of the Californios, which began in the 1820s, failed to survive the arrival of Americans from the East in 1846.

SVANEVIK & BURGETT COLLECTION

44

Soldier-explorer-politician John C. Fremont was one of numerous distinguished visitors to the home of Francisco Sanchez.

Years later, on January 20, 1839, Mexican governor Juan B. Alvarado granted this property, *Rancho San Pedro* consisting of 8,825 acres stretching approximately six miles along the ocean front from San Francisco to Montara Mountain, to the distinguished *Californio*, Francisco Sanchez. The grant was given him as a reward for past services and to assure Don Francisco's future loyalty. During the 1830s, the San Jose-born Sanchez had become prominent as a soldier and government official in both San Jose and Yerba Buena. Francisco Sanchez had been given the command of a token garrison of soldiers in the San Francisco Presidio. Later, from 1842-1843, he served as *alcalde* (mayor) of Yerba Buena.

Francisco Sanchez was the most prestigious son of the celebrated Mexican *ranchero* José Antonio Sanchez, owner of *Rancho Buri Buri*, 15,000 acres on San Mateo County's bay side. Don Francisco acquired *Rancho San Pedro* in 1839. Three years later he commenced construction of the stately adobe dwelling presently on the site. The structure was built on the foundation of the no longer existent mission *asistencia*. Walls are three feet thick. The home, well-planned and elegant by Old California standards, had three rooms on each of its two floors. The structure, shaded by tall trees, was not completed until 1846, the first year of American occupation of California.

Built on an east-west axis, this home, twenty-two feet wide and sixty-four feet in length, afforded its occupants a magnificent view of the Montara mountains. The structure occupied the precise site of the old Spanish chapel and, archaeologists have surmised, may well have been constructed with some of the original adobe bricks.

Typical of *Californios*, Don Francisco used the land for raising livestock. Throughout the 1850s, there were at least a thousand head of cattle, hundreds of horses and untold numbers of sheep grazing on the land.

The distinguished Don Francisco was said to have been well-respected by the American conquerors. Subsequently, he entertained a number at the home. One, famed soldier Captain John C. Fremont, accompanied by American Vice-Consul William Leidesdorff, noted that on a trip from San Francisco to Monterey, the pair became disoriented in dense fog while riding south from Mission Dolores. After aimlessly wandering a considerable distance and hearing the barking of dogs, they found themselves at *Rancho San Pedro* where Don Francisco offered comfortable beds, hot food and the traditional bounteous Mexican *Californio* hospitality for which the region had become so well-known.

Don Francisco died at age fifty-seven in 1862, following a fall from a troublesome horse. His widow maintained the property for a decade. Thereafter, the structure was used as a home and for a variety of other purposes. Late in the 1880s, it bore the sign "Hotel San Pedro." Its amenities were touted in San Francisco newspapers, highlighting nearby sea bathing, fishing, hunting, and

This adobe, completed in 1846, was the home of Californio Francisco Sanchez.

Above: For three decades after the 1890s, the Sanchez home served as a hotel for travelers.

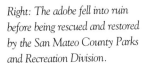

Right: The adobe fell into ruin before being rescued and restored by the San Mateo County Parks and Recreation Division.

unsurpassed climate. Adjacent to the adobe was a stable for the rental of riding horses. The hotel, which became increasingly a combination of Mexican and Victorian architecture, operated until about 1920.

During Prohibition years of the 1920s, "Adobe House," as it was then called, became a notorious speakeasy. Illegal stills lay hidden in nearby artichoke fields. The following decade, the gradually deteriorating structure was used as a lodging for farm workers. And, during the 1940s, artichoke growers turned it into a packing shed.

The adobe and five acres were sold to the county in 1947 for $7,500. Restoration was undertaken by the San Mateo County Parks and Recreation Department in 1953 to rebuild crumbling walls, banisters, sagging balconies, and return the house to its original form. Before the slow and painstaking restoration was completed, the cost was $50,000.

Had Don Francisco been present, he no doubt would have been puzzled by the care with which painters first coated the restored balcony and banisters with creosote and then with white paint to make the pieces look old. Indeed, originally Sanchez had painted the place a gleaming white in order that it appear new.

Wood frame additions, which had been appended to the house in the post-Sanchez era, along with an interior staircase, chimney and fireplace were removed. Adobe walls were reinforced with steel rods. Original outside stairs were restored and a redwood shingled roof was replaced with split cedar shingles.

In recent years, the house, one of the finest early adobes still existent in California, has been restored and furnished with attractive nineteenth-century pieces. It is open to the public as a local history and house museum under the auspices of the San Mateo County Historical Association, which is reponsible for interpretive programming. The Park Department is in charge of maintaining the house and its approximately five-and-a-half acres. Many of the eucalyptus trees planted in the late nineteenth century have been removed; cypress trees, however, dating from a much earlier era are still on the grounds.

This adobe was listed as California Historical Landmark No. 391 in 1953 and included on the National Register of Historic Places in 1976.

In addition to the county's many park units, until the 1970s, the parks department also had the responsibility to maintain and supervise nine coastal beaches, from Thornton at Daly City in the north to *Arroyo de los Frijoles* (Bean Hollow) near Half Moon Bay in the south.

However, much to the later dissatisfaction of park director Shaw along with a number of park officials (who believed that the state did not follow through on its covenant to maintain the coastal areas adequately), these beaches were turned over to the control of the state of California.

One outstanding ocean beach park, what is presently the James V. Fitzgerald Marine Reserve (originally the Moss

SAN MATEO COUNTY PARKS & RECREATION DIVISION

At low tide, the reef at Moss Beach provides visitors with a rare display of marine life forms.

Beach Marine Reserve), totaling 195 acres, was maintained. This area, three miles long and 1,000 feet deep bordered by Moss Beach in the north to Pillar Point in the south, was believed to have been first inhibited approximately 6,000-7,000 years ago. The aboriginal diets consisted primarily of turban snails, mussels, barnacles, chitons and fish gathered from the offshore reef. In addition, natives killed rabbits, black-tailed deer, and often harbor seals that accommodatingly gamboled about in the shallows and sunned themselves on the beach. Indians commonly used rabbit skins for clothing.

During the early 1880s, the land, consisting of a broad sandy beach, was acquired by Juergen F. Weinke (1844-1920), a German immigrant. At low tide, Weinke observed a rocky intertidal region cut by many channels. It contained tide pools, protected lagoons, and numerous ledges with overhanging sides. The environment, perhaps the most biologically diverse along the Pacific Coast, offered a multitude of habitats to hundreds of species of plants and animals. There were sea stars, snails, sea slugs, and tiny crabs by the thousands. Indeed, it possesses one of the greatest concentrations of intertidal life in the world in terms of different species.

Recognizing the value of this tremendous resource, parks director Shaw, in 1969, was determined to hire a professional. He chose veteran San Mateo County Ranger and Naturalist Robert Breen, a marine biologist. Breen observes that

approximately 400 types of animal life have been identified in the reef but believes that there are, in fact, hundreds more. There are probably 500 different forms of plant life.

During his initial inspection of the area in the nineteenth century, Juergen Weinke had observed unique algae growing on the rocks. He termed this vegetation *moss*. As a result, that portion of the coast later became referred to as Moss Beach. Believing that the area had the potential of becoming a health spa and major vacation attraction for San Franciscans, Weinke undertook construction of the Moss Beach Hotel. Adding to the already diverse natural vegetation of the area, Weinke ordered the planting of thousands of cypress trees. Even though access to his hotel from San Francisco was difficult, Weinke experienced considerable prosperity. On weekends, the place was virtually always full.

While the original hotel burned in 1911, many of the cypress trees, originally planted in artistic designs, still adorn the cliffs. A second Moss Beach Hotel was subsequently erected and was a popular stopping place during the 1920s and 1930s.

As early as 1906, Charles Nye arrived in Moss Beach. He constructed a restaurant, actually on the sand. Known as The Reefs, Nye's restaurant became famed for succulent abalone dinners. Abalone was so abundant on the reef that Nye claimed he could easily gather fifty of the juicy creatures in less than a half-hour each day.

Moss Beach and the restaurant experienced a decade of even greater prosperity, beginning in 1908, when the tracks of Ocean Shore Railroad were laid across Devil's

Red Star Stage Line buses regularly brought guests to the Moss Beach Hotel during the 1920s.

TOM GRAY COLLECTION

SVANEVIK & BURGETT COLLECTION

Slide continuing south along the San Mateo County coast. On weekends, hundreds of visitors armed with sacks and buckets congregated, crawled across the slippery reef gathering unique rocks to adorn their home gardens in addition to harvesting delicate sea stars and other marine creatures merely for curiosity or delicacies to add to their tables. For these folks, abalone dinner at The Reefs was an attraction that few could deny themselves. (Until 1997, when California declared a ten-year moratorium on abalone gathering, 2,700 scuba-equipped hunters a year swarmed into the Fitzgerald Marine Reserve.)

The significance of the area wasn't lost on scholars. During the 1920s, marine biologists, notably Professor S.F. Light from the University of California, were bringing classes to study the reef's many life forms and to collect intertidal invertebrates.

At that time, living accommodations along the still remote San Mateo coast were few and far between. Commonly, university students were allowed to camp on the floor of The Reefs. This successful, albeit not necessarily comfortable, arrangement was brought to an abrupt and violent conclusion in 1931 when especially high tides, coupled with a series of vicious Pacific storms battered the restaurant, ultimately reducing it to kindling. The Reefs was subsequently rebuilt in Moss Beach, this time a safe distance from the unpredictable surf.

Beginning in the 1930s and continuing for almost forty years, in their efforts to illustrate natural history, school teachers, with training in the biological sciences, brought thousands of youngsters from greater San Francisco Peninsula schools to Moss Beach.

These children obediently swarmed across the rocks, inspecting the living reef at low tide. Traditionally, they would carry buckets or bags in which to collect specimens they found to take back to school for later study. Apparently no consideration was given to the immeasurable environmental damage that was being wrought.

Contributing to this looming environmental disaster at Moss Beach during the 1960s, the hills adjacent to the beach became a popular hangout for motorcyclists. Not only did the shore become a receptacle for their waste, but at low tide bikers raced along the hard-packed sand, doing irreparable damage to wildlife.

Left: Tide pools at Moss Beach have been appreciated by scholars for decades. The Reefs, a resort and restaurant directly on the beach and an early landmark, was destroyed by a Pacific storm in 1931.

49

Moss Beach, what became the
Fitzgerald Marine Reserve, was
acquired by the county in 1969.

incidents where people were apprehended attempting to remove intertidal life either for food or merely amusement. He remembers one particularly flagrant violation when an individual pried forty-two sea stars from the rocks. The person's intent was to boil and dry them. Ultimately they were to be used to adorn the wall of his family room.

Under Breen's stewardship, the numbers of such violations have fallen dramatically. In the year 1999, there were only twenty-one recorded. Miscreants are cited under Code 10666 of California Fish and Game regulations.

Finally, San Mateo County park officials awakened to the realization that their marine resources were being rapidly destroyed. In April 1969, what later became the reserve was acquired by Parks and Recreation Department. Only in November that year, however, when it was given official reserve status, did it become illegal for visitors to remove anything from the beach and tide pools. Line fishing and the gathering of abalone were still permitted.

This desecration came to an end in November when Ranger Bob Breen, with a degree in marine biology from San Francisco State University, a former biologist with the California Academy of Sciences, was hired as the marine reserve's first naturalist.

Breen, still the supervisor at the reserve, vividly recalls that, during his first year on duty, there were more than 800

The marine conservatory was named the James V. Fitzgerald Marine Reserve in honor of the president of the San Mateo County Board of Supervisors during the 1960s. Fitzgerald, a resident of San Bruno since 1948, who, as a young man, had harvested abalone off the reef at Moss Beach, was instrumental in winning the protected status.

Adding to the already unique nature of this natural marine sanctuary, since 1995, Ranger Breen has transformed it into a living classroom for biology students enrolled at nearby Half Moon Bay High School.

Twice each week he teaches advanced placement biology to twenty-eight students who are carefully screened from the approximately eighty who apply annually. The fall semester is devoted purely to academic work. In addition to classroom and book work, there are six, two-hour field trips to Fitzgerald. In the spring, each student conducts twenty hours of discovery walks. By the end of the year, they have led approximately 4,000 elementary school-aged youngsters through the reserve.

While the most wanton destruction of Moss Beach ended with its designation and protection as a reserve, the invertebrate population of the reef has recovered only slightly. Today, greater numbers than ever before visit the reserve annually. Much of the conservation effort that came about with laws against collecting, has been nullified by the greater numbers of specimens inadvertently trampled.

Nevertheless, for students and natural history aficionados, the Fitzgerald Marine Reserve remains a place of wonder. Classes from nearby Skyline College are frequent visitors. In the area between the water and salt marshes, visitors encounter sea lions, harbor seals, and shore birds of

many varieties. The marsh is inhabited by rodents, reptiles and rabbits.

Although the population is small, visitors in summer who watch vigilantly are often privileged to catch a rare glimpse of the California sea otter, now an endangered species. Perhaps as many as twenty-two of these distinguished critters inhabit local waters, crawling up on kelp beds or rocks within the reserve to preen themselves.

Otters also provide the reserve a very important service. These gentle, albeit ravenous little animals, have a special appetite for sea urchins. As the otter population declined over decades, the numbers of sea urchins, thus unchecked, increased, presenting a real danger to kelp forests. Sea urchins multiply at such a rate that they can easily destroy a kelp bed by stripping it of its vegetation. Though the resurgence of the otter population has been slow, it assures that the numbers of always hungry sea urchins will be controlled.

Below left: Rangers guide thousands each year through the Fitzgerald Reserve displaying examples of marine life. Here, the topic is the red rock crab.

Below right: The Gumboat chiton, the largest chiton in the world, is one of hundreds of specimens frequently seen at the Marine Reserve. This specimen is shown upside down displaying the portion of the creature that clings to the rocks.

Two public trout farms operated in what is today San Pedro Valley Park. They were destroyed by floods during the 1960s. The rough terrain in the background is characteristic of the park.

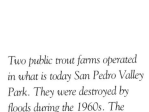

Not all of San Mateo County's parks are equally well-known or present the same broad appeal to the public. Nevertheless, three are special jewels — San Pedro Valley, Junipero Serra, and Edgewood Natural Preserve. Each adds unique luster to the diverse system.

San Pedro Valley County Park, 1,140 acres in the Linda Mar section of Pacifica, east of the Sanchez Adobe, was acquired by the county during the 1970s and developed as a park the following decade. Fifty percent of the land was purchased and the remaining fifty percent is on long-term lease to the county.

"It's a fantastic park where the animals know no bounds," states County Ranger Steven J. Durkin, who grew up in the Linda Mar area of Pacifica and who presently lives in a house on the park grounds.

Without question, the park is distinctive. Its thousand acres of meadows, hills and streams have something for everybody. There are short, easy walks, as well as challenging climbs to the ridges. Planners never intended it for recreational activities such as football, baseball or mammoth company picnics. Instead it is natural, a rich assemblage of plants, ferns, horsetails, and club mosses that are simply not found in drier inland locations.

SAN MATEO COUNTY PARKS & RECREATION DIVISION

Though now with approximately ten miles of hiking trails, the rugged setting, through coastal scrub and chaparral, is largely the same as it was when first encountered by the soldiers of Spanish Captain Gaspar de Portolá, who camped there in 1769, during the first land exploration of California. While most of the expedition's participants remained in what is today San Pedro Valley Park, Sergeant José Ortega and a detachment of men ascended nearby Sweeney Ridge. From that summit, in early November, these men became the first Europeans to discover the existence of San Francisco Bay.

San Pedro Creek, which winds down the north slope of Montara Mountain, is shaded and cool. Unlike most creeks in the county, this one flows year-round. The creek provides a stable environment for fish, insects and algae. Such populations cannot be established when a stream dries up. "A stable stream results in a stable population of plants and animals," reports Edmund Wodehouse, formerly professor of biology at nearby Skyline College.

The park's supervising ranger, Michael W. Fritz, adds that the creek is still populated by silvery-gray steelhead trout, often two feet in length. Despite a sizable human population density between the park and the ocean, these elegant fish somehow manage to swim through backyards and up stream to spawning grounds in the fresh water creek where the young are hatched.

That the fish have survived is thanks in large part to County Ranger Jesse Gilley, who, as supervisor of San Pedro Valley during the 1980s, conducted a major creek cleanup project. "We pulled debris from the creek all the way to the ocean. Backyards butted up against the creek. Many residents had commonly dumped lawn clippings and garden waste into it for years," reports Gilley.

"Creating an even larger problem, at one point the town of Pacifica had destroyed a bridge and pieces of broken concrete littered and partially blocked the creek, generating a major obstacle for the fish. We pulled it all out and undid, in a day, this awful problem that had been in the making for a decade."

The estimated number of steelhead that made it up the creek in 1983 was fifteen. Eighty made it the year after the cleanup and more than 300 three years later. Vigilance by rangers, county game wardens, and San Pedro Park volunteers, who continually maintain watch against poachers, have made it possible for increasing numbers of steelhead to return from the sea each year to spawn.

Feeding into San Pedro Creek is Brooks Creek, reached via a narrow and rugged trail. At least during winter months, there is a three-tiered, cascading waterfall of 175 feet. Over the years, this has become a favorite haunt of photographers.

During the 1950s and 1960s, before the area became part of the parks department, it was known for two trout farms where local residents came to fish. These ceased to exist after extensive damage caused by flooding in 1962.

Of all the county parks, San Pedro Valley receives a tremendous amount of local use. As many as 120,000 people annually make use of the dirt and graveled trails and limited picnic facilities. It is a favorite sanctuary for hikers. "Even on the wettest and coldest days of winter," notes Fritz, "the faithful regulars still are seen on the trails."

These folks have become exceedingly comfortable with the diverse wildlife, notably black-tailed deer, coyotes, gray foxes, and solitary bobcats, easily noted because of their facial ruff and pointed ears tipped with tufts of black hair.

Park administrators, Area Managers Kendall Simmons and Bob Emert, were photographed in 1976 while they toured Junipero Serra Park.

Providing some of the most spectacular vistas of San Francisco Bay and the entire Peninsula is Junipero Serra County Park, a 108-acre piece of wooded land in the hills behind the city of San Bruno. Its entry is from Crystal Springs

Road between Skyline Boulevard and Interstate 280. The Serra Fault, a secondary earthquake fault branching off from the more major San Andreas, rips through the park. The land on which the park exists was once a portion of *Rancho Buri Buri*. Later, it became part of the property of Comstock millionaire and San Francisco banker Darius Ogden Mills.

This property, the advantages of which were first recognized by parks director Shaw in the 1950s, was once known as the North County Park. Shaw had identified the need for new facilities in the northern part of the county and moved to acquire it. The land was purchased by the county in 1956. "Shaw drew the plan for Junipero Serra on a napkin while sitting at his kitchen table," relates Jesse Gilley. The land was dedicated as a county park May 22, 1960. In 1971 alone, more than 400,000 visitors made use of the facilities.

The park has proved to be especially popular, probably because of its proximity to the freeway and easy access from most parts of the Peninsula and San Francisco. Users especially appreciate the variation in the foliage; there are pines and eucalyptus on the hills and below, the meadows are punctuated with elegant oaks.

Careful observers find evidence of the hunters and gatherers who comprised the Peninsula's aboriginal population, before the arrival of the Spaniards. Skeletal remains of five Native Americans and evidence of three Indian cremations have been found there. Shell mounds have been located in the lower elevations of the park. Not long ago, during leveling for a new trail, several mortars and pestles, used by local natives hundreds of years ago, were uncovered. Every summer Stanford University archaeology professor

PHOTOGRAPH BY SUSAN SOMMERS

Patrick Hunt brings students, as part of a four-week seminar, to excavate a section of the park little known to the public. Native artifacts which have been found, including arrowheads and pestles, are displayed in glass cases in the park office.

Left: Edgewood County Park and Natural Preserve became noted for its deposits of serpentine rock, which inhibits weeds, thus allowing native wildflowers to flourish.

Offering a radically different environment is Edgewood County Park and Natural Preserve, a 467-acre expanse in the hills west of Redwood City. Edgewood is known for its serpentine soil, low in calcium and nitrogen but high in magnesium and heavy metals, which rejects most non-native species, therefore, allowing native wildflowers to florish. Edgewood is one of the unique areas of the state for its biological diversity.

Some carefully planted non-native trees, however, offer evidence that Edgewood has not always been a park. At least portions were originally developed for residential use.

The first modern resident and the builder of a home in what is presently the park was John Isaac, a 49-year-old Englishman who arrived in San Mateo County in 1891. Three years later, planning to build a home for his bride, at the close of California Midwinter International Exposition in Golden Gate Park (1894), Isaac purchased one of the exhibition structures, the Monterey Building.

Isaac traded the roofing tiles from that building (made originally during the late eighteenth century for *Mission San*

SVANEVIK & BURGETT COLLECTION

Above: The Henry Finklers built one of the first homes in what is today Edgewood Park. Among other accomplishments, Finkler was known for his scientific study of Peninsula climate.

Right: Edgewood Park is also known for its amazing variety of bird life. Pictured is the Western meadowlark.

PHOTOGRAPH BY SUSAN SOMMERS

Below: San Mateo thornmint, once thought to be extinct, was found among the tremendous variety of plants and flowers flourishing at Edgewood Park.

Antonio de Padua, in the hills east of Carmel) to Southern Pacific Railroad for use on the Burlingame railroad depot then under construction. In return, Southern Pacific had the building dismantled and brought to Redwood City by train. Sections of the structure were dragged by horses to the spot where Isaac chose to build (near the present-day amphitheater). There, amid the trees and wildflowers, the new owner erected a spacious two-story structure for his family.

The Isaac family maintained the property until 1903 when it was sold to Henry C. Finkler, a man of proud Prussian ancestry who later became secretary to the California Supreme Court.

Upon moving to Redwood City, Finkler developed an almost neurotic obsession with what he considered to be the region's outstanding climate. With Prussian precision, he set about meticulously gathering and recording weather statistics. Dissatisfied with merely collecting data, Finkler, for a decade, corresponded with foreign governments in the effort to compile comparative figures.

In that Finkler, as far as is known, made the only such climate studies of the San Francisco Peninsula, his family came to believe that his data was later used as the basis for Redwood City's claim that the region's climate "was best by government test." Finkler moved out of the big house after the death of his wife in 1927, choosing to live in a smaller home on the property. He became increasingly despondent and committed suicide on the property November 18, 1930.

Years later, in 1967, in search of land for construction of a state college on the San Francisco Peninsula, California officials exercised the state's right of eminent domain, purchasing the site for $4 million. The property was acquired for the projected Edgewood Hills State College. When this idea fell through, the state abandoned the land in 1979. Thereafter, the Edgewood site was purchased in 1980 by San Mateo County for $2.3 million. The old home was demolished. The county announced plans for the construction of a golf course.

PHOTOGRAPH BY SUSAN SOMMERS

Biologists and botanists, who revere the park's 160 acres of serpentine grassland and have discovered a harmonious concentration of ecological zones, opposed the idea of a golf course. In terms of biological riches, Edgewood County Park and Natural Preserve is looked upon by many as the "Fort Knox of the Bay Area." Scientists view it as a living museum with a biological window to California's past. They believed that a golf course of any size would do irreparable damage to the unique plant communities existent within the bounds of the property.

The park, dominated by a ridge, includes magnificent tree-shaded, fern-filled canyons. Especially during the period from January to May, Edgewood is acclaimed for its spring splendor. Elegant wildflower-bedecked meadows create variegated vistas of color. Cool, wooded gullies are rich in ferns and mosses.

Approximately 480 different plants have been identified. Seventy-five percent of these are natives. Two species are endangered: *San Mateo thornmint* (until recently considered extinct) and the *white-rayed pentachaeta*.

Wildlife in the park is also abundant. Identified have been seventy resident and migratory birds. There are frequent sightings of deer, raccoons, bobcats, coyotes, rattlesnakes and other small animals. Edgewood boasts being host to the state rock (serpentine), the state flower (poppy), and the state bird (quail).

BAY CHECKERSPOT BUTTERFLY

Adult butterflies emerge from cocoons in spring and feed on a number of plants which thrive in serpentine soil. These butterflies mate and lay eggs during a season that lasts between four and six weeks. It is believed that females mate only once but males do so multiple times. Females can lay up to 1,000 eggs. For both sexes, the average life span is ten days.

One of the few colonies of the Bay checkerspot butterfly still existent is situated in Edgewood Park.

PHOTOGRAPH BY SUSAN SOMMERS

Above: Susán Sommers was one of the first to discover the uniqueness of the land that became Edgewood County Park and Natural Preserve. She led a twenty-five-year effort to save land.

Right: Many of the hills and meadows now part of Edgewood Park were virtually destroyed by off-road vehicles before the machines were ultimately banned by the county.

Edgewood is also a habitat for the rare and endangered dark brown-, orange-, and cream-colored *checkerspot butterfly* (Euphydryas editha bayensis). Colonies of this fragile butterfly have been found only in this park, on Jaspar Ridge and on San Bruno Mountain

Susán Sommers, today of Hillsborough, first saw the Edgewood property in 1969. "I'd always been interested in both nature and wildlife and had gotten involved in plant identification." At Edgewood, she looked across "a wonderful display," seemingly endless fields of wildflowers. Her realization was almost instantaneous. She clearly understood what neither the Sierra Club nor San Mateo County park officials had yet grasped. From the standpoint of nature, Edgewood was something of incredible value and she set out to make people aware of it.

"I had no special background; I was just Joe Citizen," Sommers remarks. Nevertheless, she embarked on a twenty-five year, often lonesome, crusade to save the property. Not infrequently regarded as a "troublemaker" by county officials and those who championed another golf course, she worked constantly, talking to anyone who would listen. Ultimately a Save Edgewood Park Coalition was formed. This dedicated group was composed of more than fifty environmentally interested organizations. Today, Edgewood County Park and Natural Preserve, exists as a monument both to the solitary efforts of Sommers and to the steadfast determination of the coalition.

One of her first crusades was to rid Edgewood of off-road vehicles that began to desecrate the land during the early 1980s. The region was not patrolled by police and a lot of drivers found Edgewood was a great place for four-wheelers to play. "I vividly remember one Saturday when there were almost 300 vehicles cutting up the landscape…. Today, the damage is still being repaired," states Sommers. "Off-trail mountain bikes also became a major problem." Finally, all were effectively banished by the county.

Even though consultants who had undertaken one study of the area for the county had concluded there was "nothing of environmental value" at Edgewood, Sommers began her

58

plant identification process. Over the years, she has conclusively identified hundreds of species of plants and wildflowers. Early in the 1970s, the California Native Plant Society was formed. "I checked my list against theirs and realized that several plants in the park were endangered."

Sommers also mounted what became a protracted struggle against the county's plan to use a portion of the land to build an eighteen-hole golf course. "They planned to lower the hills by carting off 270,000 cubic yards of valuable serpentine soil," she states while shaking her head incredulously.

Her dogged efforts finally paid off. A 15,000-signature petition calling upon the Board of Supervisors to protect Edgewood Park was presented. In May 1992, responding to concerns of environmentalists, supervisors recommended that the park become a *natural preserve* and receive protection from the threat of future development. This was accomplished in May 1993. Edgewood Park is the only *natural preserve* in San Mateo County.

"This is God's country. I can't believe that they pay me to be here," states County Ranger Priscilla Alvarez while deftly negotiating Huddart Park's approximately twenty miles of hiking and riding trails in a park department-owned, four-wheel drive Jeep. Gesturing toward the forest, she adds: "This is why I became a ranger."

Huddart Park in Woodside is celebrated for its steep slopes and stately groves of trees.

PHOTOGRAPH BY SHIRLEY BURGETT

59

Right: Millionaire lumberman James M. Huddart offered his property to San Francisco and California before it was finally accepted by San Mateo County.

Below: Assistant Park Superintendent and Ranger David Moore was photographed standing at the AIDS Memorial Grove at Huddart Park. The memorial was placed there in October 1997.

Alvarez, a young San Francisco-born Hispanic woman, who before being assigned to Huddart Park in 1989 had served seven years as a ranger at Coyote Point, is convinced that 973-acre Huddart, is the quintessential county park. "All I need to make it absolutely perfect," she says smiling, "is a trout pond…then I would never have to go on vacation."

Located in Woodside on the east slope of the Sierra Morena with entry off of Kings Mountain Road, Huddart Park offers spectacular views of the surrounding countryside. Most of the park is heavily forested with coast redwoods,

Douglas firs and ancient oaks. Distinguishing features of Huddart are the park's steep slopes and deep, dark, fern-filled canyons where the sun seldom, if ever, shines and it is perpetually cool. Meanwhile, higher up in the grassy meadowlands, where, during summertime temperatures often skyrocket past a hundred degrees, profusions of colorful wildflowers and wild iris bloom in spring.

Lumberjacks invaded what is today the park area during the California Gold Rush of the 1850s, methodically hacking out Douglas fir and old-growth coast redwoods. Visitors to the park still see cut-off redwood stumps, monuments of yesteryear, today surrounded by circles of new growth, "fairy rings" as they commonly are known.

The manner in which San Mateo acquired this valuable expanse of property was convoluted at best. It had been owned by multi-millionaire San Francisco lumberman and longtime Woodside resident James M. Huddart. During the 1930s, part of the initial acreage had been sold to James Flood, grandson of silver titan James C. Flood. After the sale in 1934 of *Linden Towers*, Flood's sprawling Menlo Park estate, the family moved to Greer Road in Woodside. That

massive, gabled-roofed Flood home can still be seen from several vantage points in Huddart Park meadowlands.

James Huddart died March 31, 1935. By the provisions of his will, the remainder of his property was bequeathed to the City and County of San Francisco. He added, however, if San Francisco failed to accept it, the land was to go to the state for use as a park. Upon acquisition, California also held the property for two years until, concluding that maintaining the land created greater difficulties than the state was willing to undertake. At that point, the property was donated to San Mateo County. Because it apparently was not served by adequate water, county officials considered rejecting the gift as well. However, after journalist Raymond Spangler, editor-publisher of the *Redwood City Tribune*, dug through records and determined that the county did in fact have water rights, the gift was enthusiastically accepted. Huddart County Park opened in 1948.

San Mateo County Fire Warden Bert Werder had convinced the Board of Supervisors that the land was ideal for use by youth groups. And in so doing, he had been extremely instrumental in the ultimate acquisition of the property. Thereafter, Werder laid out the first system of hiking and riding trails. When the park opened, it primarily served youth activities, notably the Boy Scouts, who were the first regular campers. In May 1952, 600 Boy Scouts convened there. Because of Werder's contribution, the first family picnic area in the park, dedicated in May 1954, was named for him.

Over the years, eighty acres of the park have been developed for picnicking and public camping. Approximately 200,000 people annually use the park.

FAIRY RINGS

Horticultural specialists argue over the true age of coast redwoods (*Sequoia sempervirens*). Some contend that the stately trees possess all the ingredients of immortality. When burned, damaged, or cut, a tree refuses to die but almost immediately sends out, from its root ball, a great thicket of new sprouts. These form a circle of young trees (fairy rings) around the base of the parent stem.

New growths comprise a second generation of the parent tree, which is genetically unchanged. Therefore, though a circle of trees may be only a few decades old, it is possible that the subterranean root ball is ancient. Given the nature of these trees, concludes writer John Hart, coast redwoods may be the "oldest living woody plant in the world."

Second generation trees are gradually reduced in number by competition. Young redwoods don't share the same invincibility as their older relatives. Succulent young redwood shoots are especially attractive to gray squirrels and black-tailed deer.

A madrone curling skyward toward the light in Wunderlich Park.

Connected to Huddart, via a five mile-long stretch of the Skyline Trail, is 942-acre Wunderlich County Park, probably the most ecologically diverse unit east of Skyline Boulevard. It is primarily woodland and is well-watered with a large number of springs. "Perhaps none of the county's parks is as rich in human history," states Ranger Charles Brock, who served there for a decade after 1978. Except for the area immediately around an old stable near the park entrance (along Highway 84), there has been little development.

Unlike Huddart, which is ideal for both camping and day use, Wunderlich offers little; there are no barbecue grills, picnic areas, or campgrounds. Alambique Creek runs diagonally across the park. There are perhaps fifteen miles of hiking and riding trails winding through meadows and a steep evergreen forest mixed with coyote brush. Most of these trails were developed after the property was acquired by the county.

This "rough and ready" park is especially popular with equestrians. Patrick Henry Sanchez, named to be director of the San Mateo County parks in September 1993, always referred to Wunderlich as "the county's best kept secret."

Many notable county names are associated with the property. During the 1840s, Mexican Governor Juan Bautista Alvarado granted Irish-born pioneer John Coppinger a

62

12,500-acre expanse, then called *Rancho Cañada de Raymundo*. Coppinger, one of the first non-hispanic Europeans to live on the Peninsula, built a dam on Bear Gulch Creek and erected an adobe dwelling. Subsequently, in 1846, 2,880 acres of that land were deeded to early county lumberman Charles Brown who referred to it as *Mountain Home Ranch*.

Evidence of the logging era is abundant. Two well-preserved skid roads, side by side, down which oxen slid the great logs during the 1850s and 1860s, are still distinguishable. With ruts between five and ten feet deep, they begin near Skyline Boulevard and end very close to Woodside Road. There were probably no actual mills in what is today Wunderlich Park. Only two old-growth coast redwoods remain. One, on Alambique Trail, is approximately fourteen feet in diameter; the other, not especially tall, is close to Skyline Boulevard.

John Coffee Hays, the first sheriff of San Francisco County, who had gained notoriety as a Texas Ranger before coming to California during the Gold Rush, acquired the property in 1850. He called it simply the *Hays Ranch*. While Hays lived on the property, he commuted to San Francisco daily on horseback.[9]

A generation later after several other lesser known owners briefly held the property, in 1872, the western portion comprising 1,500 acres was sold to importer and exporter Simon L. Jones, who maintained offices in San Francisco and

ILLUSTRATED HISTORY OF SAN MATEO COUNTY, CALIFORNIA (1878)

Hazel Wood Farm, the property of Simon L. Jones, as depicted in the 1870s by lithographers Moore and DePue.

Hong Kong. Before coming to California, like Hays, Jones had gained prominence as a Texas Ranger.

Employing gangs of Chinese laborers, Jones undertook the clearing of brush and trees on the cut over land to develop a working ranch. Jones called his spread *Hazel Wood Farm*. Visitors today may still see rotting remains of redwood wagon bridges along with pieces of a moss-covered, decaying grape-stake fence, all erected by Jones more than a century ago.

Jones cross-fenced the property to graze cattle and horses. As an ardent agriculturalist, he planted a vineyard to produce raisins and fruit orchards including prunes and apples. In the year 1886 alone, he exported 14,000 pounds of raisins to China.

Additionally Jones introduced a number of other non-native trees. Thus, besides the traditional native specimens, the park is known for stands of Monterey cypress, olive, and eucalyptus trees. While serving as windbreaks, the fast-

---

[9]*Until the Consolidation Act by the state legislature in 1856, the city of San Francisco and the entire Peninsula as far south as San Francisquito Creek comprised the legal jurisdiction known as San Francisco County.*

Right: James A. Folger II, scion of the coffee millionaire, finished this Edwardian home in 1906. The house itself was never part of Wunderlich Park.

PHOTOGRAPH BY BILL WARTO

Below: Huddart Park Ranger Priscillia Alvarez inspects the former Folger carriage house presently in Wunderlich Park. For a time this structure served as the park office.

PHOTOGRAPH BY SHIRLEY BURGETT

growing eucalyptus trees were planted almost exclusively to assure Jones a ready supply of firewood.

Among the farm's attractions were sulphur springs which bubbled forth from crevices in apparently solid rock. The rocks were coated with white sulphur and the area was odorous with sulphur fumes. Many local residents drank the water, firmly believing that it had medicinal qualities.

Nearby was a spring of natural gas.

Simon L. Jones died in August 1890. For a dozen years the property was farmed by his son Everett who moved there with his wife and two children. In October 1902, young Jones sold *Hazel Wood Farm* to James A. Folger II. The new owner, scion of the Gold Rush coffee pioneer, renamed the estate *Hazelwood Hills*.

At the time, *Hazelwood Hills*, an expanse of almost 2,000 acres (extending from Bear Gulch Road to La Honda Road and from Woodside Road to Skyline), was Folger's summer retreat. The family used it frequently for carriage trips, excursions, camp outs in the woods, and as a place of general rustication away from San Francisco. Recently, the site of Folger's skeet range has been located. The area is still littered with pieces of broken clay pigeons.

The Folgers continued Jones' agricultural pursuits, planting cherries, apples, and pears. Some of the original apple trees still bear fruit. County Ranger Brock believes he personally harvested the last of the Folger pears, a single piece of fruit that ripened in 1977.

Folger ordered construction of a magnificent family house to be designed by renowned San Francisco architect Arthur Brown Jr. It was under construction and damaged (two chimneys fell) during the earthquake of 1906. While the big house was being built, the Folgers occupied the older Jones dwelling.

The new house, a grand four-storied structure, celebrated for its Edwardian flourishes and characterized by awning-shaded windows, is still extant. This luxurious mansion typified the transformation of the Woodside area from a logging region to a place of elegant country living for San Francisco's landed gentry. The home is located just outside of Wunderlich Park. Nevertheless, it can be seen from various points in the park.[10]

In addition to the big house, Folger also maintained a campsite near Alambique Flat. Several tent frames with wooden platforms were scattered on the flat. Canvas was put over the frames when in use. Mrs. Folger and the children

used tents when the family needed a true vacation. In 1927, after the death of her husband, Mrs. Folger ordered a small vacation cabin built there.

Less than a half-mile west of the main house, in 1905, Folger erected a two-story, redwood-sided, cupolaed stable, also designed by architect Arthur Brown Jr. This extraordinary structure, complete with deep roof, dormers, and porte-cochere, is often described as Victorian Gothic.

Originally heated by three huge brick fireplaces, the stable was highlighted by a cobblestone floor and pink marble base panels. Interior walls are of redwood paneling laboriously stained to resemble mahogany. Doors are wrought iron over glass. Gas chandeliers, said to have been especially luxurious, have long since been removed. The stable building, still famed for its decorative elements, is currently leased to a private party and used commercially as a boarding stable.

Typical of other great landowners of his era, Folger used his property primarily for horse breeding. Additionally, Folger harnessed the waters of nearby Alambique Creek, storing it in a 100- by 50-foot concrete reservoir near Salamander Flat. The water was used to create the area's first hydro-electric power. His was said to have been the original house on the Peninsula fully wired for electricity. Folger also powered a sawmill constructed on the property.

The Folger family sold most of the estate, with the exception of the house, to contractor Martin Wunderlich in 1956. Wunderlich, a native of Denmark, intended to subdivide the land, but these plans were short-circuited. Although plans were made, it was determined that because of the proximity of the San Andreas fault, the land was

---

[10]In 1976, the Folger house was sold to Nolan Bushnell who had made an extraordinary fortune in video games as the founder of the Atari Company and creator to the first Pong Game. Bushnell paid just over $500,000 for the house and invested millions restoring it to its pristine elegance. Terraced gardens along with stairways and paths were also restored. Bushnell was celebrated for his lavish entertainment that attracted participants from all over the world. Parties often continued for several days. For the pleasure of his guests, an array of video games were installed in the garret. Late in the 1970s, Bushnell was married in the house. The home and thirteen acres subsequently sold to venture capitalist Jonathan Carol, in 1998, for $5.5 million. At that time, Bushnell was near bankruptcy.

extremely unstable and given to sliding. There was also the matter of Wunderlich's declining health. In 1974, two years before his death, Wunderlich deeded the 942-acre expanse to the San Mateo County for use as a park.

At the time of the acquisition, within the bounds of the park were the old Simon L. Jones home, a Folger carriage house, and the 1905 stable. All were earmarked for preservation.

The ultimate fate of the Jones house, badly in need of repair, was a subject for debate. Many wanted it torn down. Others, recognizing its historical value, pleaded that it be saved. But in 1975 the controversy abruptly ended when an overzealous county-paid contractor, who, by himself and without explanation, appeared on the property one morning before dawn, bulldozed the antique structure.

Thereafter, the carriage house, with much of the same architectural detailing as the stable, was for some years used as the park headquarters.

Right: Ranger Tom Baker, a longtime veteran of the Memorial Pescadero Creek Park Complex, is presently assigned to windy San Bruno Mountain State and County Park.

"The fragrance is better than Kauai," exclaimed one recent visitor to San Bruno Mountain State & County Park, as she sniffed the perfumed aroma of the many diverse spring wildflowers wafting up the hill's steep slopes.

"And," responded Supervising County Park Ranger Ronald S. Weaver, as he regarded the dramatic panorama of the Peninsula spread out below, "on clear days you can see all the way to Albuquerque."

Perhaps something of a good-natured exaggeration, but it indeed seems that way. Tough winds can be counted on to be

PHOTOGRAPH BY SHIRLEY BURGETT

blustery and dense fog is a common visitor; there is no better place on the Peninsula for 360-degree views; most agree that they cannot be duplicated. Even when foggy, the marine layer is often low enough that sun continues to shine on the brooding summit and in the distance. Looking over the tombstones of Colma, the vista of the vast Pacific and the Farrallon Islands, thirty-one miles to the west, is breathtaking. One's line of sight to the east is interrupted only by distant mountain chains.

Parks director Shaw, during the 1960s, was probably one of the first to recognize naked San Bruno Mountain in North San Mateo County as an ideal place for the creation of a regional park.

This "island amongst the urban sprawl," borders on Daly City, Brisbane, South San Francisco, and Colma. San Bruno Mountain rises starkly from sea level to an elevation of 1,314 feet. Other than the fact that San Bruno Mountain is an impressive feature on the horizon and that it is the site of frequent brushfires during the dry season, relatively few people on the San Francisco Peninsula are aware of its genuine uniqueness. In fact, according to Harvard University biologist E.O. Wilson, there is more biological diversity on San Bruno Mountain than in the Costa Rican rain forest.

Perhaps only those who fly above it during take-off from San Francisco International Airport (located just seven miles to the south) even begin to acquire some small appreciation of just how dramatic the mountain is. Its dark summit bristles with radio and television towers and saucers.

The vast expanse of almost 3,600 acres is characterized by dwarf manzanita clinging to steep, grassy slopes and rugged ridges. The mountain is also cut by deep, dramatic valleys. And while most of the land is covered with annual grasses and typical coastal scrub vegetation, it is also punctuated by sylvan glades, dense clusters of eucalyptus planted during the nineteenth century, and weathered clumps of Monterey cypress.

Irregular topography of the mountain creates microclimates, producing dramatic fluctuations of temperature at any given time. While the northwestern part of the mountain is experiencing damp foggy conditions, the southeastern slopes can be sunny and warm. Typically, temperatures vary from a low of forty degrees fahrenheit to

This early view of San Bruno Mountain from the old Reichhardt's Duck Farm in Colma shows the mountain as it appeared before development of the summit.

highs in the mid-eighties. Kamchatka Point was named after a place in Siberia because of the extreme cold and windy conditions usually associated with this outcropping.

Even in the warmest weather, gusting winds near the summit are chilling. Ranger Ron Weaver, who holds degrees in life sciences and zoology, comments that the park gives special meaning to the Mark Twain quip: "The coldest winter I ever spent was summer in San Francisco." At greatest velocity, wind speeds on the summit can reach eighty miles per hour. Rainfall on the mountain averages between twenty and twenty-five inches annually.

Who, early in the 1960s, could have guessed that the mountain, for two decades, would become a major battleground between environmentalists and big business? Looking back on the controversy, it appears to have been easier and quicker for the United States government to find a solution to the war in Vietnam.

On the one side were wealthy developers who, understanding the genuine housing shortages that existed on the San Francisco Peninsula, recognized the almost unlimited homebuilding potential of the mountain. Opposing them were conservationists who cherished the mountain as an ecological treasure. They were determined that it remain open space.

The line was drawn in 1960s when the Crocker Land Company,[11] owners of the mountain, in association with the Ideal Cement Company of Denver and David Rockefeller, president of the Chase Manhattan Bank in New York City, began publicly discussing their plans for the development of what they referred to as Visitacion Rancho property. Representatives of these companies predicted that by the end of the twentieth century, they would complete a billion dollar development. Their intention was to construct 36,000 new homes to accommodate a population of up to more than 100,000 people.

This proposal, in part, was the removal of the entire crown of the mountain to lower the summit. Approximately 350 million cubic yards of earth would be moved by a sophisticated conveyor belt from the mountaintop and dumped into the bay to provide fill for the expansion of the San Francisco International Airport and a possible southern crossing of the bay. Had this plan gone into effect, thirty square miles of tideland and open water would have been erased, creating a landfill roughly the size of New York's Manhattan Island. "The enormous scale of the Crocker plan was just incredible," stated planner Harry Dean. "Had they tried this ten years before, they probably would have gotten away with it."

---

[11]*During the Spanish and Mexican eras of California history, San Bruno Mountain was used for the grazing of cattle and sheep. A 3,814-acre expanse, including all of San Bruno Mountain, was acquired by multi-millionaire transcontinental railroad-builder Charles Crocker in 1884. After his death, the property passed to the control of the Crocker Estate Company, and in 1891, to the Crocker Land Company.*

Leveled off, development could have proceeded with greater ease. Crocker's proposal was to reduce available park land to a mere fifty-eight acres.

Crocker Land Company was not prepared for the opposition to its proposal. Almost immediately, Ralph Shaw called for the establishment of a 300-400 acre regional park on the northwest side of the mountain near Daly City.

Then, in 1968, came the book, The *Flora of San Bruno Mountain* by Walter Knight and Elizabeth McClintock. Therein the authors, both of the California Academy of Sciences, identified 384 specific species of plant life existent on the mountain in addition to more than fifty varieties of grass. The four-mile-long mountain was an "ecological island" supporting unique communities of plants and animals. The mountain was identified as one of the most important and threatened biologically diverse sites in the United States.

The book provided evidence of rare and endangered species. Fourteen species of the mountain's plants fit into this category. Several of the seventeen species of manzanita that have been identified are unique to the mountain.

Insect life was also studied. There are four species of rare and endangered or threatened butterflies. High atop the mountain, scientists found two tiny species of caterpillars hibernating in rodent burrows and ant nests. Every spring,

these caterpillars blossom into rare butterflies for about two weeks before dying.

These were the almost extinct Mission Blue Butterfly (*Plebejus icariodes missionensis*), which is widely distributed through the grasslands of the mountain in two major colonies, and the San Bruno Elfin Butterfly (*Incinsalia fotis bayensis*); there are fourteen colonies of the San Bruno Elfin on the north-facing slopes of the main ridge.

Two other species, the Callippe Silverspot Butterfly (*Speyeria callippe callippe*) and the Bay Checkerspot Butterfly (*Occidryas editha bayensis*) are listed as threatened.

And, to the delight of biologists, it was discovered that San Bruno Mountain was also the habitat for the San Francisco Garter Snake (*Thamnophis sirtalis tetrataenia*), which is listed on both the state and federal endangered lists.

Park Planner Harry Dean (right) and Ranger Ron Weaver are beginning the arduous task of laying out trails on rugged San Bruno Mountain.

Barely had the plans of the Crocker Land Company been publicly unveiled than a grassroots effort was undertaken by citizens in surrounding communities to stymie them.

Bette Higgins of South San Francisco could look out the front window of her modest home and gaze at the bare side of San Bruno Mountain. So upset was she by the proposal, that Higgins vowed then and there that development would not be completed without a fight. She became the proverbial tiger on Crocker's tail and the epitome of all those who contended that development constituted a vicious rape of the environment.

Therewith, the determined Higgins formed the Committee to Save San Bruno Mountain. It was the beginning of an energized citizenry that found leaders in Ellie Larson and David Schooley. Before this volunteer enterprise met ultimately with success, it had been joined by the Sierra Club, Audubon Society, and a number of other environmentally committed groups. These people were adamantly determined to resist housing and commercial development on the mountain by having the land acquired for a regional park. Seldom has a citizen's group been as effective in terms of thwarting the grandiose ambitions of big business.

"It was the committee's grassroots effort that resulted in broad county and regional support," declared an obviously delighted San Mateo County Parks and Recreation Director David Christy while attending the dedication of the new regional park in 1986.

After protracted negotiations between San Mateo County and developers, in 1978, the county agreed to buy 1,165 acres. Park director Duane "Doc" Mattison, who had coveted San Bruno Mountain since the 1950s when he had served as park and recreation director of South San Francisco, presented Crocker Land Company a check for $6.2 million.

Almost simultaneously, a further agreement was reached that permitted a much scaled down and severely limited development of the mountain. In return, Crocker Land Company donated an additional 564 acres to the county. This allowed the county to plan a regional park of approximately 1,711 acres, thus covering almost half of the 3,500 acre mountain.

For $5.2 million, the state of California, in 1980, purchased the 297-acre saddle of the mountain. Although this was to remain state property, by a ninety-nine-year operating agreement, it was placed under management of the San Mateo County Parks Division. Smaller land gifts subsequently brought the park to 2,266 acres. The county was offered the opportunity to purchase the crown of the mountain for an additional $6 million. This was declined. As a result, the summit is presently owned by the American Tower Company. Several hundred additional acres were acquired by the county in 1980. San Bruno Mountain State & County Park currently is 2,400 acres. Though earmarked for inclusion in the park, a Native American burial ground on the east slope of the mountain close to Bayshore Freeway will one day come under the park's jurisdiction. Ultimately, the park will be approximately 3,000 acres.

Longtime County Parks Commissioner Nita Spangler declared in 1986 that the Save San Bruno Mountain project was a "genuine triumph for citizen participation." Indeed, few local grassroots efforts have ever been crowned with such amazing success. The brooding peak, once sarcastically referred to as "that worthless rock" and as "Mattison's Mountain," can truly be viewed as a "people's park."

Unfortunately, the victory wasn't so great as conservationists had hoped and as it initially appeared it would be. In fact, it was actually something short of total. The federal Endangered Species Act of the 1970s prohibits the killing or injuring of any endangered species. If animals, butterflies, or other endangered critters are threatened on public or private land, no development can be undertaken.

But in 1982, as a result of the San Bruno Mountain upheaval, this landmark piece of legislation was amended to allow some development if a Habitat Conservation Plan (HCP) were prepared.

This amendment provided for a limited amount of development within an endangered habitat if a developer agrees to trade or preserve other property providing a similar and protected environment. And landowners who acquire property in such an area are required to pay a certain amount annually. This money becomes a source of funding to conserve and maintain remaining habitats to prevent the extinction of a species. The money also is meant to ensure the ongoing preservation and maintenance of these habitats.

San Mateo County Supervisor Anna Eshoo tossing out the "first frisbee" at the dedication of San Bruno Mountain State and County Park in 1986.

SAN MATEO COUNTY PARKS & RECREATION DIVISION

PHOTOGRAPHS BY SHIRLEY BURGETT

Especially during spring, San Bruno Mountain is renowned for its amazing array of wildflowers. Pictured are the California poppy (top left), the crimson or hummingbird sage (top right), Reddened clarkia (bottom left), and the wild iris (bottom right).

Under these provisions of the HCP, developers of the mountain were allowed to develop approximately 368 acres from private open land while adding over 800 acres to the park.

San Bruno Mountain is another marvelous example of biological diversity. The park offers one of the most spectacular wildflower displays in the state. During spring, the wildflower display is similar in numbers and uniqueness to the one at Edgewood County Park but it is different in the species that bloom.

Non-native plants were already starting to invade areas of the park when it was placed under the protection of the HCP. The activities and amount of funding available during the past two decades to implement the plan have not stopped the march of these exotic plants. The funding picture doesn't look any better in the future and volunteers are stepping in to work on habitat protection. While the park is protected, it is still unclear whether the habitat protection originally envisioned by the authors of the legislative amendment will ever be realized.

Few of the 60,000 to 70,000 annual visitors to San Bruno Mountain State & County Park leave disappointed. While the trails have not been constructed to accommodate either horses or bicycles, "our twelve miles of hiking trails are tough to beat," exclaims the always boyish and enthusiastic Ranger Ron Weaver.

Visitors, who generally reflect the multi-ethnic nature of the communities surrounding the mountain, return frequently either to hike or to follow the continually changing wildflower panorama. The bone-chilling winds serve to discourage use by day campers and picnickers.[12]

Often, visitors from foreign lands come only once. Their visits to the mountain top are usually limited to a few minutes. They come merely to appreciate the breathtaking vistas of the Bay Area below.

---

[12]*Initial trails and public access to San Bruno Mountain were provided by an eight-person California Employment and Training Act (CETA) team, the 1980s version of the federal Works Progress Administration (WPA).*

While native flowers, including California poppies and lupine, grow in abundance, their existence is increasingly threatened, not by development but by invasive non-native plants. Most notably, the thorned Scottish yellow gorse, albeit magnificent to look upon in spring, is invading valuable grassland.

Militarily, San Bruno Mountain played a strategic role in the history of the area. U.S. Army Signal Corps forces occupied it during World War II, establishing a signaling operation in a small cluster of buildings in the saddle area. Aircraft searchlight, capable of illuminating the skies in case of air attack, were also installed near the summit.

Military forces returned in 1956, during the Cold War, to construct a Nike radar missile site just below the summit on the west peak facing toward the ocean. Radars and ignition devices were placed atop the mountain, although the missiles themselves had been emplaced at Fort Funston (nearby on the coast) and on Milagra Ridge above Pacifica. The press of a button on San Bruno Mountain and anti-aircraft missiles would have fired instantly.

The missile complex was deactivated in 1963. The government sold the buildings to the Crocker Land Company for the munificent sum of $1. Today those buildings serve as the park's headquarters corporation yard.

Motorists who have driven Alpine Road between Pescadero and La Honda[13] surely will quickly recognize the name Emanuel B. McDonald, or Sam McDonald as the man was better known.

In 1917, McDonald acquired a homesite on what eventually became 430 acres of steep redwoods near La Honda. There, "among the lords of the forest," he built

The summit of San Bruno Mountain served as the control center for a NIKE anti-aircraft missile site during the Cold War. It was deactivated in 1963. The buildings presently serve as the ranger station for the park.

---

[13]*Late nineteenth-century travel guides listed La Honda as the most attractive picnic and camping area on the Peninsula. "Nowhere in the world can you find a more beautiful spot. The village is a favorite retreat and summer resort with its noble redwood forest, fairy-like dells, sparkling brooks; and, in the upper reaches, its rolling hills, orchards…and flower bedecked meadows. During summer, hundreds of campers spread their tents beneath the shady trees. Far enough from the ocean to avoid the damp fogs, La Honda's climate is unequaled."*

PHOTOGRAPH BY SHIRLEY BURGETT

THE SAN MATEO COUNTY RANGER

In May 1998, Lynne Fritz was promoted, becoming the division's first woman to hold the position of Superintendent of Parks.

Originally, during the 1930s, park rangers were simply called attendants. In 1962, they were reclassified as "park rangers." Not until 1977 were they given badges and limited law enforcement responsibilities. At that time, parks director "Doc" Mattison was given the first badge. Thereafter, all park directors have carried Badge No. 1.

"Rangers are the last of the good guys who wear uniforms…they don't carry guns," reports Robert Emert. "With the public, they still have a wholesome Smokey the Bear image …rangers are probably the last bastion of acceptable authority to people."

There are both men and women rangers. The first permanent woman ranger, Badge No. 52, Lynne Weaver Fritz, joined the department in 1979. Since then, she has served at every park except Wunderlich and Coyote Point Marina. In May 1998, Fritz was promoted to the position of park superintendent. She resigned from the department in August 2000 to accept a ranger position nearer to her family in the Sierra foothills.

"San Mateo is one of the few counties in the state where rangers are expected to be generalists," reports assistant parks superintendent Dave Moore. Rangers are supposed to be jacks-of-all-trades, experts at everything from building picnic tables to laying out trails or getting involved in sophisticated forest management.

Steven J. Durkin, one of the county's forty-eight uniformed rangers (in 2000), has no difficulty with the job description. He loves what he does and is proud to wear the gold badge of a San Mateo County Park Ranger. It seemed like the natural thing for him to do. "I grew up out-of-doors in Pacifica with a 2,000-foot granite cliff at our back door. San Pedro Valley Park was my old stomping ground. Weekend camping at County Memorial Park was the family's favorite form of recreation."

Since first employed as a seasonal ranger in 1980, Durkin has worked in eight of the park units. "I welcome new challenges and the different environments," he remarks.

Presently, Durkin is assigned with Ranger Bob Breen at the Fitzgerald Marine Reserve, a popular park visited by 130,000 people in 1997 alone. Durkin particularly enjoys interpretive work. "We deal with people of all ages…I talk to different groups from kindergartners to college graduate students."

Durkin, whose college training had concentrated primarily in geology, is now increasingly involved in marine biology. His interests have evolved and he contemplates returning to college for formal training to better equip him for this position. Meanwhile, he works with the community as the vice-president of a chapter of the American Cetacean Society and a volunteer in the Gulf of the Farallones National Marine Society. He maintains liaison with The California Marine Mammal Center and the Academy of Sciences.

It quickly becomes apparent, while hiking with Durkin along the narrow sandy beach at the reserve, that a ranger is more than a cop, more than a janitor, and more than a forester. He is a steward of the resources and caretaker of the land.

At least for now, the ocean is Durkin's world. He delights discussing the reef while identifying its life forms. He explains how erosion of the bluffs, caused by the vicious storms of 1998, revealed two fossilized ribs from a now extinct baleen whale which, dead or dying, had become buried in the mudstone there somewhere between three and five million years ago. (The skull of the whale and one other rib had been discovered before Durkin was assigned to Fitzgerald. The skull is presently being displayed at the California Academy of Sciences in Golden Gate Park.)

Durkin, who lives in ranger quarters at San Pedro Valley Park, has found each of his assignments fascinating. One highlight, he recalls, occurred in 1993 while he was at Sawyer Camp Trail. The ranger was asked by the Society for the Prevention of Cruelty to Animals to assist in returning a red-tailed hawk to the wilds. Upon release, near Crystal Springs Lake, the stately bird, which had recovered in captivity from a gunshot wound, rose magnificently from his box and flew off to the watershed. The incident seemed to exemplify, at least for Durkin, what being a county ranger is all about.

County Ranger Steven Durkin points out fossilized remains of a pre-historic whale presently imbedded in the cliff at Fitzgerald Marine Reserve.

PHOTOGRAPH BY SHIRLEY BURGETT

Sam McDonald, Stanford University's grounds superintendent, bought his first piece of property near La Honda in 1917.

himself a "humble retreat," a log lodge that he named *Chee-Chee-Wa-Wa* (meaning "little squirrel"). The place contained several bedrooms, a kitchen, and a living room with a spacious porch overlooking Alpine Creek, which he dammed to allow his guests the opportunity to splash about in the icy water. The son of a Methodist minister, McDonald said he used "this temple of nature" for prayer, meditation, and reflection.

In his forest sanctuary, he also established the *La Honda-Alpine-Ytaioa Reserve* "to afford asylum to all wild creatures." Local inhabitants and visitors alike firmly understood that upon this reserve, neither deer nor lowly wood rat was ever to be disturbed. Cutting of trees was not permitted.

Among the redwoods, the six-foot-four-inch McDonald spent virtually all of his vacations and summer weekends. Weather permitting, he frequently drove up after work. La Honda residents came almost to depend upon him; even on the wettest winter weekends, they saw him pass through town.

He buzzed around the village in his Ford Model A, becoming one of the town's best-known and liked personalities. (Retired County Parks Ranger Gary Woodhams, a lifelong resident of La Honda, vividly remembers Sam McDonald and his Ford Model A. "He kept that old car well into the 1950s and used it to drive around the roads that were cut on his property.") McDonald informed townsfolk that he respected the serenity and isolation of the forest.

Perhaps, by themselves, these few facts are not especially important. Add to them, however, the fact that Sam

McDonald was born January 1, 1884, in Monroe, Louisiana, the son of former slaves. He then suddenly becomes an intriguing personality.

For many years, this big African American was the only person of color to own property in the redwoods and was one of the better known and most popular men on the Stanford University campus.

McDonald's long association with Stanford University began in 1903, when, at age nineteen, he was hired to haul gravel from San Francisquito Creek for the maintenance of campus roads. Not long thereafter, when university officials declared war on student drinking, McDonald was hired as a "night watchman" to keep order in the men's dormitory. When he was on duty, drinking was never a problem.

The job for which he was best known, superintendent of athletic buildings and grounds, he was given in 1908. From then until his retirement, with twenty subordinates, he was in charge of sports fields, tennis courts, tracks, and boat houses.

McDonald acquired a reputation for creating the best turf in the West. In 1921, when Stanford completed its new football stadium, McDonald not only planted sturdy turf, he worked out a new method of mowing alternate sections between yard stripes so that they appeared to be planted with different types of grass.

McDonald was well-connected and maintained a close relationship with former United States Senator Samuel Shortridge, a conservative Republican from Atherton. Late in the senator's life they became fast friends and visited with one another regularly. McDonald also maintained a friendship with former President Herbert Hoover and both knew and corresponded with David Starr Jordan, Stanford University's founding president.

In May 1941, then Stanford president Ray Lyman Wilbur named a thoroughfare on the campus *Sam McDonald Road*. Wilbur declared that McDonald was probably better known and liked than any faculty member, administrator or student on the campus. "I'm glad I don't have to run against Sam for office; I would fear the result." Wilbur concluded that aside from doing good work, McDonald perhaps hosted the best barbecues in the state.

California Governor Goodwin J. Knight, in 1954, a Stanford graduate himself, dropped by McDonald's university office just "to shoot the breeze and discuss old times."

The congenial Sam was devoted to students, especially athletes who came to revere him as the impresario of the barbecue. On the coast at Miramar Beach, at Searsville Lake, or amid the redwoods at *Chee-Chee-Wa-Wa* on Alpine Creek, he was forever putting on outdoor feeds for the baseball, track, or football squads. McDonald's open-air lamb roasts at La Honda for university faculty and administrators and his less formal feeds for Stanford athletes, who continually "tested my ability in the art of sizzling meat over the barbecue pit," were always much anticipated events. University president or student, an invitation to *Chee-Chee-Wa-Wa* was never to be ignored. It has been estimated that, through the years, Sam barbecued literally for thousands.

Stanford students who got married often honeymooned in Sam McDonald's cottage. In later years, McDonald gave the Sierra Club permission to use the property to conduct hiking classes.

To this day at Stanford Convalescent Hospital, although McDonald died in 1957, his name, at least among the medical staff, has become legendary. "The children of the hospital are my family," declared McDonald, a lifelong bachelor. For fifty years, he was every child's unofficial grandfather. He spent most of his Thanksgivings and Christmases with the kids.

During World War II, when evergreen Christmas trees became difficult commodities to find, McDonald hiked his property in La Honda choosing "perfect trees" to be decorated by the children at the hospital.

Chee-Chee-Wa-Wa, McDonald's forest cottage, was badly damaged by floods of the 1990s. It is presently being restored.

McDonald and friends from Stanford making mirth at the cottage in the redwoods.

Perhaps not surprisingly, when McDonald died in November 1957, he bequeathed *Chee-Chee-Wa-Wa* and 430 acres of property in the redwoods of La Honda to the Stanford Convalescent Hospital. With no immediate use for the gift, the following year, for $67,000, the university sold the land to San Mateo County. It was to be used as a park.[14]

"Sam McDonald Day" was first celebrated in 1920 and held every May thereafter. That day Stanford students swarmed the Convalescent Hospital to paint, work the gardens and visit with sick children. Traditionally, the day concluded with a fund-raising picnic with McDonald as chef.

Upon McDonald's retirement from Stanford after more than fifty years of unbroken employment, university President J.E. Wallace Sterling, presented him with a new automobile. He had broken all records for length of service at Stanford.

San Mateo County Parks Director Ralph Shaw served as master of ceremonies for the dedication of Sam McDonald Park, August 27, 1970. Given McDonald's appreciation of young people, it seemed right that the colors were presented by Boy Scouts.

The park, now almost 900 acres with the addition, in 1976, of the adjacent Kendall B. "Pete" Towne property, is on steep, rough terrain. It is situated along both sides of Pescadero Road, approximately three miles west of La Honda. Elevations are 300 to 1,300 feet at Towne Ridge. The ridge provides spectacular vistas of the Butano and Skyline ridges as well as the Pacific Ocean.

"McDonald is too steep to be a traditional park," states Bob Emert who was assigned as the park's first supervising ranger in 1970. The difficult terrain and miles of steep trail have given Sam McDonald the reputation as being a hikers' park. "Our program was to provide a successful first and second experience in backpacking," remarks Emert, "but as a

---

[14]*Few individuals were ever better loved on the Stanford University campus than Sam McDonald. He attended every Big Game for fifty years. McDonald died in November 1957. The Big Game was played several weeks later on November 24. At half time, the Stanford Band, instead of forming into the traditional axe, grouped into the letters S-A-M and played the Stanford hymn in his honor. Then a Stanford card stunt spelled out: "In memory of Sam."*

park for the masses it isn't." Nevertheless, the trails are revered by horsemen. Probably the ruggedness of the park contributes to the fact that it is not as heavily used as many of the other parks.

The vast acreage is forested with sixty-year-old, second-growth coast redwoods, interspersed with a few first-growth that remain. These heritage trees are approximately fifteen feet in diameter. Redwoods are mixed with Douglas fir, other evergreens and meadowland. In spring, during and after the rainy season, McDonald Park abounds with lush mosses, curious mushrooms, and colorful displays of wildflowers.

Today Sam McDonald is one segment of the Memorial-Pescadero Creek Park Complex. Of these components, Sam McDonald is known as the greenest and as the park where the vegetation is probably thickest.

It had been McDonald's wish that his property be maintained for and used by young people. Appropriately today, notes longtime County Ranger Tom O'Connor, there are three youth camps in the park. Groups that use them are required to backpack in, often more than a mile from the parking area (one vehicle per group is permitted inside the park for emergencies).

At the youth camps, only the basics are provided. There are restrooms, barbecue grills, and a campfire pit. Cold water is available but there is absolutely no electricity. "The park is not as heavily utilized as it could be," remarked Harry Dean, "but there are not a lot of things for kids to do when they get there."

After Sam McDonald Park was established, *Chee-Chee-Wa-Wa*, McDonald's original home, was maintained for use as

a residence for park rangers. It continued to serve until 1998 when major flooding along Alpine Creek did great damage to the structure. "Some people thought we should destroy it," remarks Memorial-Pescadero Creek Park's supervising ranger, John Kenney. "But I could not bring myself to wreck it." The old home, explains Kenney, will be lifted onto a new foundation and be used once more.

During the rainy season, wild mushrooms of many varieties spring up on the forest floor. While some are edible, most are poisonous and deadly.

SAN MATEO COUNTY PARKS & RECREATION DIVISION

Right: This wooden path through Heritage Grove protects the forest floor and the shallow root systems of the coast redwoods.

Below: Heritage Grove, perhaps the last grove of virgin coast redwoods visible from the highway, was dedicated in 1980.

Most of the large old-growth redwoods in San Mateo County had been logged out by 1900. There were of course a few notable exceptions. One magnificent grove, along Alpine Road a mile west of Pescadero Road, was on thirty-seven acres adjoining Sam McDonald Park to the northeast.

That these ancient trees had miraculously been spared was largely due to the determination of Jane Rodgers who lived on the property. In 1966, however, that land was sold to the Holmes Lumber Company.

Grace Anne Radwell, a local resident who lived in a "semi-primitive cabin" on Alpine Creek near La Honda, had special appreciation for the area. "We called it Shangri-La in summer and Pneumonia Gulch in winter," she explains.

Now a resident of Half Moon Bay, Grace Radwell vividly recalls her appreciation of the huge trees and her absolute indignation on the day when she drove along Alpine Road and saw that the trees had been slashed with blue paint. These magnificent giants were scheduled for cutting. Radwell was not a joiner and didn't belong to any kind of environmental

SAN MATEO COUNTY PARKS & RECREATION DIVISION

SAN MATEO COUNTY PARKS & RECREATION DIVISION

organization. Nevertheless, she proclaims, "I couldn't and wouldn't allow this to happen." Holmes Lumber Company wasn't prepared for Mrs. Radwell.

Early in the 1970s she formed a citizens' group to stop the destruction. The first substantial donation came from Big Creek Lumber Company. In short order, Radwell enlisted the support of twenty-six environmental organizations. "It was a very popular drive," she states, "for a year, I did nothing but eat, sleep, and save trees." Before the drive was over "we literally had bushel baskets full of money…and every cent we raised went toward the trees."

This was unquestionably the finest grove of old-growth redwoods remaining along a San Mateo County road and thus easily accessible to residents. Some of the trees rose to the dizzying height of 280 feet and were twelve feet in diameter. A few experts felt that these eloquent giants were more perfect than those in Big Basin State Park. Some, estimated at 1,500 years old, had been growing since the fall of the Roman Empire.

Holmes Lumber placed a price tag of $190,000 on the trees. Radwell launched into an unprecedented countywide effort to raise $80,000 to pay for the citizens' share of the thirty-seven-acre parcel. "Before allocating county funds, the supervisors wanted to gauge the extent of community commitment," remarked County Ranger Tom Baker who spent twenty years in the Memorial-Pescadero Creek Park Complex.

The amazing effort was ultimately crowned with success. On July 25, 1974, the San Mateo County Board of Supervisors put up the remainder of the money to purchase the trees. Thereafter, this small piece of land has been known as Heritage Grove Redwood Preserve.

Shortly before the purchase, Parks Director Jack Brook was asked what the county intended to do with it. His response was: "We'll leave it exactly as it is."

San Mateo County officials had great expectations for the land, in July 1968, when they acquired 4,736 forested acres in a rugged and barely accessible part of the south county between Memorial Park and Portola State Park.[15]

Logging had gone on in this area since the mid-1850s when John Tuffley built the first sawmill on Pescadero Creek, approximately four miles upstream from the town. Such operations have continued intermittently ever since. The heaviest logging, extensive clear-cutting, had been between the 1920s and the 1950s when a narrow gauge steam train hauled timbers to the mill.

Creating what became a complicated situation, at the time of the purchase by the county, the acquisition included only the trees under twenty-four inches in diameter. Indeed,

---

[15]*During the earliest years of American settlement, this area was part of Santa Cruz County, although it was virtually inaccessible from Santa Cruz. By an act of the California legislature in 1868, the land was transferred to San Mateo County.*

Park volunteers have engaged in a myriad of tasks that could not have been accomplished without them. This book represents one of the projects undertaken by volunteers at the Fitzgerald Marine Reserve.

The
Natural History
of the
Fitzgerald Marine Reserve

Published by the
Friends of Fitzgerald Marine Life Refuge

INTREPID VOLUNTEERS

Volunteer coordinator and Ranger Nick Ramirez grew up in the North Beach neighborhood of San Francisco and graduated from Galileo High School.

When he came to work for San Mateo County in 1978, the parks presented a new and special world to him. Since then, he has served as a ranger in all of the county units, with the exception of Memorial and the Fitzgerald Marine Reserve.

Long before accepting the position of volunteer coordinator in 1998, Ramirez had come to have an appreciation for the approximately 350 individuals who serve regularly as volunteers. "They come from all walks of life …and help preserve and enhance the park habitats and trails."

It is almost impossible to stereotype the volunteer. Some are Boy Scouts. Others come from local churches or are retired adults. And yet others are

students from schools in the area. "A few teachers give credit for volunteer service," Ramirez explains. An increasing number of businesses — Oracle, for example — are becoming involved. What all volunteers have in common is their love of the outdoors.

Volunteers are respected and admired by park professionals. Some wear the same khaki shirts and patches as the county rangers. "Many park users can't tell the difference between the volunteers and the pros," adds Ramirez.

Specialists with the Native Plant Society have noted that California is presently losing far more acreage to weeds than to suburban development. On any given weekend members of the California Native Plant Society and Friends of Edgewood Natural Preserve, all volunteers under the watchful eye of Supervising Ranger Ricardo Trejo, will be on hands and knees meticulously removing non-native plants and weeds that threaten that wildflower wonderland. Simultaneously, at Moss Beach, Friends of the Fitzgerald Marine Reserve (formed in 1985) are busy cataloging specimens. Meanwhile, among the redwoods at Huddart Park, volunteers rake trails and clean culverts. At San Bruno Mountain and in San Pedro Valley parks, volunteer organizations are teaching environmental education.

PHOTOGRAPH BY A.E. WIESLANDER, U.S. FOREST SERVICE

Volunteer groups take part in literally hundreds of different activities. Of all such organizations, perhaps the oldest is the Volunteer Horse Patrol, which, since the 1980s, has assisted rangers patrolling the hundreds of miles of trail in all the equestrian parks.

Riding their own horses, volunteers, who are equipped with two-way radios, enhance the pleasure of park users by assisting disoriented hikers. "Where does this trail go?" is the question most commonly posed to volunteers, states Marian VandenBosch, longtime member of the patrol. Volunteers also report on fallen trees, washouts, and unusual animal sightings. Each of the approximately ninety riders has been fully trained in first-aid techniques.

Looking back at the year 1999, Ranger John Kenney noted that the total number of hours contributed just by the Horse Patrol, at the Memorial-Pescadero Park Complex, was 2,496. At the in-kind volunteer rate of $20.00 per hour, their services amounted to $49,920. Throughout the park system for the year 1999, 1,947 volunteers performed 16,360 hours of labor. It is estimated that this contribution was worth well more than a quarter million dollars, unquestionably a significant contribution to the Parks and Recreation Department.

Santa Cruz Lumber Company retained cutting rights of the larger specimen and was continuing to log. The county took an option to later purchase larger trees for stumpage (the value of a tree before it is cut).

Not long after the transaction to acquire the land, the San Mateo County Sheriff's Honor Farm was moved onto a portion of the property. The compound was established at Camp Pomponio, the former Boy Scout campground. Prisoners from the minimum security prison were to assist the lumber company clear the land of slash.[16]

Haphazard logging operations in the Memorial-Pescadero Creek Park Complex. This damage to the terrain occurred during the 1930s when there was little thought of conservation.

---

[16]*The Sheriff's Honor Camp has become a permanent fixture in Pescadero Creek Park. It is a city in itself, including barracks for prisoners, a mess hall, sewer plant and administration building. The camp has an independent water system. Food is trucked in. While the compound is fenced, this is a minimum security facility; there are no armed guards or towers. As part of their rehabilitation program, prisoners do invaluable work for the county, especially in the Memorial-Pescadero Creek Park complex. While other parks may use prisoner labor, the long commute to and from the compound reduces the feasibility.*

This abandoned sawmill was photographed during the 1930s near the Memorial-Pescadero Creek Park Complex.

This original acquisition, with additional smaller purchases, ultimately amounted to 5,700 acres. The county's intent had not been to establish another park but to construct a 400-foot-high dam (in the area of Worley Flat) to be built by the U.S. Army Corps of Engineers. Such a barrier, engineers reported, would create a massive reservoir more than seven miles in length and approximately two miles in width. At its deepest point, there would be almost seventy feet of water.

There was a legitimate rationale behind the plan. Engineers saw it as a method of providing flood control along Pescadero Creek and a means to assure coastside residents of a continual supply of water; there would be an adequate supply for coastside farmers to irrigate their fields. Had this plan been executed, planners envisioned that sleepy Pescadero would become a booming city of 70,000. Additionally, the proposed lake would also serve county residents for boating and other recreational purposes.

But barely had plans become known than the proposed dam slammed into overwhelming opposition. Environmentalists were outraged at the potential destruction of the forest. The state of California was also alarmed. When filled, the dam would create a lake so large, its waters would inundate much of Portola State Park, laying ruin to at least some of that park's most stately redwood groves. County planner Harry Dean Jr. later recalled that the San Mateo County Board of Supervisors simply was not ready for the population buildup that would result along the Coastside.

"All told," comments Emert, "environmentally it was not acceptable." In short order, the dam project was shelved and county officials began to create plans for the development of Pescadero Creek Park.

But even this was not accomplished without major difficulty. The land was acquired in 1968; Santa Cruz Lumber continued to log the forest until 1971 with the intention of clear-cutting all trees below 400 feet. Emert remarks: "So now we had to purchase trees at that elevation." Faced with ever increasing costs, county officials could not afford to purchase all of the trees. Thus, they attempted to chose young healthy specimens with the classic redwood grove look.

County Ranger Tom O'Connor vividly recalls seeing Ralph Shaw in an old jeep, checkbook in hand, rumbling

SAN MATEO COUNTY PARKS & RECREATION DIVISION

through the forest choosing and tagging groves he wanted preserved. Each tree had to be purchased individually.

"Shaw did most of the work; he was a great talker," states Bob Emert admiringly. Shaw had to move fast. He was "like a kid at a candy counter; he had a dime and wanted twenty cents worth of candy," recalls Emert. "When we ran out of money, we ended up trading one grove for a better one. We were crying big alligator tears filling up the creek."

Shaw's colleagues graphically remember one grove of magnificent virgin redwoods with massive trunks. Upon first seeing them on a Friday afternoon, Shaw fell in love with the trees. He returned first thing Monday morning to buy them. "But by then," remarks O'Connor, "they were already down; Santa Cruz Lumber had logged through the weekend…. Shaw was enraged."

Development in Pescadero Creek Park has been limited primarily to the creation of trails. Access to the area is restricted to hikers and those on horseback. There are no paved roads. Pescadero Creek, which runs continuously throughout the year, flows through a steep-sloped canyon in the center of the park. Steelhead trout, responsible for attracting multitudes of sports fishermen, especially during the late nineteenth century, spawn in the creek. (According to the San Mateo County Fish and Games Protective

Left: Pescadero Creek is fed by numerous tributaries that trickle down the Sierra Morena. There is water in the creek the year-round.

85

Ranger Gary Woodhams, a resident of La Honda, spent his entire career at Memorial Park where he became something of a legend.

During the late 1960s, students at the University of California, Santa Cruz, became so enamored with banana slugs that populate their wooded campus that they adopted the marvelous mollusk as the official symbol of the university.

Association in 1904, fishermen were not permitted to take away "more than 100 fish in one calendar day." These fish are now protected. No fishing is allowed except at the ocean mouth.) From the headwaters of the Pescadero to the ocean, the distance is approximately twenty-five miles.

While much of the forest has been methodically logged, probably because of the geographic isolation, some stands of virgin coast redwoods and towering Douglas fir are still existent. Additionally, there are numerous groves of second-growth redwoods, many forming characteristic fairy rings, which rise like sentinels, protecting a fallen parent tree.

Among the most celebrated of the many creatures that inhabit the forest floor is the giant, vivid yellow banana slug, which at maturity reach six to eight inches in length. A strong sense of smell directs these slimy, albeit harmless, creatures to their food which includes living and decaying vegetation, mushrooms, seeds, roots, animal waste, and carcasses. But slug scholars note that these mollusks will choose to starve before eating shoots of young coast redwoods.

Predators of slugs have been seen to choke on the slime of the critters. Scientists have witnessed fastidious raccoons using their paws gently rolling these golden mollusks in the dirt to coat them, thus making the thick mucus more acceptable to their discerning palates.

Colorful banks of wild azaleas, rhododendrons, orchids, and an array of other wildflowers blossom in spring. On the moist forest floor where vegetation is the thickest, sun seldom shines. Mushrooms, of a thousand varieties, abound. Black-tailed deer, apparently oblivious to human invaders, roam through fields of delicate blue forget-me-nots.

The curious discover ample evidence of earlier logging operations. Skid roads, though now partly obscured by the dense vegetation, are still abundantly identifiable. Rusting cables and other pieces of abandoned logging equipment litter the forest. Also noticable are signs of a logging railroad that operated during the twentieth century. Notches in stumps reveal where, once upon a time, lumberjacks stood on springboards while cutting trees. Hikers will also find the remains of a historic sawmill where workers cut railroad ties on Tarwater Creek.

What has become known as the Memorial-Pescadero Park Complex includes Sam McDonald, Heritage Grove, Memorial, and all of Pescadero Creek Park.

Memorial Park, dedicated in 1924, is adjacent to Pescadero Creek Park on the west side. During the course of this park's more than seventy-five years, it has consistently been one of the county's most popular resorts for rustication.

"Many local residents use Memorial and it is one of the closest camping parks to San Francisco," states retired County Ranger Gary Woodhams, a resident of La Honda who was hired by the parks department in 1962 and spent his entire career at Memorial. "People really like to have a place to get away from it all…in June, the park is full every night. We never take reservations and people learn if they want to get in to arrive by Thursday." There are 158 campsites. (All of the original sites were laid out personally by Henry Bloomquist, the county's first park employee who became the first supervisor at Memorial.)

"And," adds Warren Swing, who, as a Boy Scout, camped in Memorial during the late 1920s and over the years has returned regularly, "the park itself hasn't changed at all." Swing and his wife enjoyed camping with their children when they were infants. "We still go every now and then for three or four days at a time, usually to celebrate a family birthday." Except now, when the family gathers, the children are in their forties and there are four grandchildren.

While, for a day's outing, the family usually takes off to the coast to appreciate beach and surf, Swing seldom fails to entertain the grandchildren with the colorful tales of what it was like "in the old days," when he was a Boy Scout. Like, for example, taking the test for a First Class ranking. All boys were required to swim fifty yards in the frigid waters of Pescadero Creek. "We came out like icicles."

"The same families keep coming back year after year," states Supervising Ranger John Kenney, a veteran of almost thirty years in the park system. "More than fifty percent of our campers are repeaters." Kenney, a seasoned woodsman, knows virtually every tree in the park, which is a good thing. "A lot of people return and want a particular campsite, usually the one they had last time…. We do our very best to help them find it and usually do."

There is always plenty for a family to do. Besides swimming in the creek, there is hiking, horseshoes, and

interpretive programs three evenings a week during summer. Night hikes are always popular.

Many campers who frequent Memorial Park are San Francisco or San Mateo County residents. Probably more, however, those seeking a cooling environment, drive over from the East Bay or from the Central Valley. Large numbers also head here from the Middle West. The location of the campground is ideal. It is close to beaches, close to Santa Cruz, and only forty minutes from busy San Francisco.

Rangers John Kenney and Michael Fritz as they appeared in 1976. Kenney is presently supervising ranger at Memorial Park; Fritz is supervisor at San Pedro Valley Park.

Julia Bott, executive director of the San Mateo County Parks and Recreation Foundation, meets with former Park Commissioner Nita Spangler at the 1999 rededication of Memorial Park.

Memorial has been rated as one of the top ten parks in the California. Its reputation is international. The campgrounds have become especially popular with foreign visitors. Ranger Kenney is always surprised, albeit pleased, at how many Germans, Dutch, Swiss, Japanese, and other nationalities come to the county with this park in mind. The typical length of stay at Memorial is a week.

"This is a family park," states Kenney, "and generates a lot of good feeling and good will. If Disneyland is the happiest place in California, Memorial is the next."

Kenney runs the Memorial-Pescadero Creek complex with a crew of six. But during summer when the park population often numbers in the thousands and the complex becomes a virtual outdoor city, the staff is augmented by as many as a dozen park aides, usually unmarried students.

"These kids do invaluable service. The park couldn't operate without them. Usually they become very popular with the campers," says Woodhams. "The park aides make friends and get lots of invitations for dinner; they don't end up having to buy much food."

By 1992, as government support for the county parks continued to decline and the costs of maintaining high quality faciltities for the public increased, a volunteer citizens group, ultimately what came to be called the Alternative Funding Committee, was formed. Chaired by indefatigable Park Commissioner Linda Dyson, the committee's purpose was to identify specific needs of the parks and methods of funding them. After consideration of a variety of possible solutions, it appeared to the committee that the only viable option that seemed feasible to stabliize financing was the creation of a nonprofit foundation.

The San Mateo County Parks and Recreation Foundation, with its office in the old adobe headquarters at Flood Park, began slowly. Julia Bott, a graduate of the School of Environmental Studies and Planning at Sonoma State University and the former director of the Loma Prieta Chapter of the Sierra Club, was named as the foundation's executive director in October 1998. "It took several months just getting things set up," Bott admits. "We didn't get our letter from the Internal Revenue Service allowing us to raise funds until February 1999 and couldn't even get a telephone installed for three months."

Bott and a dedicated eight-member board share a love for the county parks and a commitment to generating community support for them. "We exist to supplement the county budget, not replace it," states Bott enthusiastically. "The Board of Supervisors is very supportive and is not about to reduce the parks budget on the basis of our success."

County tax dollars are used to pay the rangers and the parks staff. Presently, tax money assures that the trails are safe, the facilities are maintained, and the restrooms are clean. "The Parks Division has done a wonderful job stretching tax dollars," says Parks and Recreation Foundation chairman Bruce Wright, "but now the foundation is out to raise money for value added amenities. Our purpose is to get people to augment tax dollars."

The foundation firmly believes in the essential role of parks in the community. Parks provide recreation, habitat, a place for people to volunteer and are an integral part of the community's history. The foundation endeavors to fund projects that address each of these elements.

During its first year, the San Mateo Parks Foundation has been enormously successful in its fundraising efforts. Just under $400,000 has been collected. "And a number of important projects have already been funded," declares an obviously delighted Bott.

Over the years, playground equipment at Flood Park had become well-worn and was not designed to current safety standards. Pam Noyer, supervising ranger at Flood declares that, "on any sunny Sunday, there might be as many as a hundred excited youngsters climbing on the equipment simultaneously."

Often, the importance of a good playground is easily overlooked. Playgrounds are supposed to be fun while generating creative thinking and developing both motor and social skills. Newly designed playground equipment has been created to provide challenges for children with all levels of abilities. One of the foundation's first grants, $125,000, was for the installation of safe new equipment at Flood Park.

Additionally, the foundation recognizes the importance of park volunteers. The parks literally cannot exist without them. Thus, an annual grant has been made to the county for the support of these generous individuals. A large portion of this money goes toward the purchase of tools and other essential equipment to make the role of the volunteer both easier and more effective.

Other first-year projects funded by the foundation included the initial phase of a vegetation management plan for the parks. This aims to assess existing vegetation, which will lead to a second plan to develop ways for performing routine maintenance, and to work out a system to eradicate invasive non-native plants. A project to improve fish habitat along Pescadero Creek in Memorial Park was also funded.

Not only did the foundation help finance the seventy-fifth anniversary and rededication exercises for Memorial County Park in 1999 but it has also supported this publication that endeavors to acquaint citizens with the variety and quality of the existent park system.

REDEDICATION OF MEMORIAL PARK

Several hundred enthusiastic San Mateo County residents, park friends, and politicians gathered in flag-bedecked Legion Flat at Memorial County Park, July 10, 1999, for the rededication and celebration of the park's seventy-fifth anniversary.

Hosted by Memorial County Park with support from the San Mateo County Parks and Recreation Foundation, the event was efficiently carried out by Ranger John Kenney and his staff. Mary Burns, San Mateo County Parks and Recreation Director, welcomed the throng. The colors were presented by the County's Horsemen's Association Color Guard.

Beneath an awning of majestic redwoods, while a bugler sounded "Taps," rangers unveiled a new bronze plaque, rededicating the park, not only to the dead of World War I but to the memory of all American soldiers who had given the ultimate gift to their country. The strains of "Amazing Grace," played by a lone bagpiper, echoed throughout the forest.

Following, at a mammoth steak and chicken barbecue served on tables beneath the trees, picnic master of ceremonies, Ranger Ron Weaver introduced Jean Cloud of Redwood City. She, the daughter-in-law of Roy W. Cloud, who had first alerted the Board of Supervisors to these magnificent stands of redwoods during the 1920s, reminisced not only about the man and his position but spoke of his steadfast determination to preserve these eloquent trees for posterity.

Helen Hickey Waddell, niece of Thomas L. Hickey, former president of the San Mateo County Board of Supervisors during the 1920s, who was often referred to as "the father of Memorial Park," told of her esteemed uncle's love of open space and especially this heavily forested wilderness sanctuary.

Friends of Memorial Park who had, over the years, consistently returned to these campsites along Pescadero Creek, told of repeated good times and warm memories.

The seventy-fifth anniversary of Memorial Park was marked with a solemn rededication July 10, 1999.

PHOTOGRAPH BY MARTY ROSE SPRINGER

The foundation's plans for the future are equally ambitious. Recognizing the historic significance of the nineteenth-century Sanchez Adobe in Pacifica, a new site plan is contemplated. "We realize the interpretive value of the site and that the existing plan is inadequate," states Bott. "We also plan to finance important rehabilitation and restoration not only of the building but the entire site."

Additionally, in the category of future projects is the planned construction of interpretive centers for Edgewood Park & Preserve, the James V. Fitzgerald Marine Reserve, and for San Bruno Mountain State and County Park.

"People often ask us why we need to erect buildings to help users enjoy the parks," reports Bott. "But that's not what we're doing. Our goal is to provide centers to support interpretive activities and thus enhance appreciation of these valuable facilities." Currently the plan is to have artist drawings of an Edgewood Interpretive Center by fall of 2001. Such projects are not inexpensive. An interpretive center can cost anywhere from $800,000 to $1.5 million.

During its inaugural year, the lion's share of the foundation's support has come from individuals. "But as we mature," adds Bott, "we want to solicit the assistance of businesses and other foundations." Such groups, however,

want to invest in going concerns. "Before approaching them, we needed to have some successes behind us."

A Recreation Commission was established under the county charter of the 1930s. However, not until the appointment of Ralph Shaw in 1945 was there a director. That title was changed in 1946 when he was made Director of Parks and Recreation.

Shaw's dedication was never doubted. He created the modern department. "At one time Shaw even mortgaged his house to pay for the acquisition of a piece of property he considered essential for the parks." He was a glad-hander, an excellent politician and a "hard-headed bulldog," remembers

Assistant Parks Director John "Jack" Brook, who succeeded Ralph Shaw as Director in 1971. Brook paused for lunch in Pescadero Creek Park in 1968.

Park Director "Doc" Mattison (standing next to truck) is photographed with planner Harry Dean and guests overlooking the Sierra Morena in 1980.

and was often required to play "the bad cop" because, states Emert, "Ralph always wanted to be the good cop."

As director (1971-1977), Brook ran a tight ship. He was thorough and a stickler for detail. Subordinates became better at writing memorandums. The director believed that the art of writing was rewriting. If a memo got past Brook without correction, it was a cause for celebration.

Brook suffered a heart attack in 1977. The following day, assistant director "Doc" Mattison became the interim chief.

Born in Nebraska, the son of a doctor, Duane Mattison was always known as "Little Doc." After a time, the nickname was shortened to "Doc." He carried that moniker around for the rest of his career. "In fact, he insisted upon it," reports Emert. "If you wanted to be more formal with him, it was "Mr. Doc."

As director (1977-1982) Mattison was eminently smooth and considered a nice guy. He was effective with the parks commission. While Brook had always striven for the full consensus of the commission, Mattison was happy with a simple majority.

Bob Emert notes that Mattison had bad knees as a result of old football injuries. Thus, he could not spend a lot of time in the field and relied heavily on reports of his subordinates. But Doc Mattison was seen enough in the

Bob Emert. During Shaw's tenure, "the parks master plan existed only in his head."

Shaw retired in 1971. In stature, Shaw had not been a large man. Nevertheless, he left behind a giant pair of shoes to fill. The director's position went to Shaw's assistant John "Jack" Brook Jr.

Brook, who grew up in Daly City, was never the same public personality that Shaw had been. Nor was he so popular. He had been hired as the harbor master at Coyote Point Marina and came up through the ranks. But, during his years as Shaw's assistant, Brook did a lot of the tedious paperwork

ROBERT S. EMERT

Few men had greater influence on the development of the San Mateo County Parks and Recreation Division than Robert S. Emert, often known around the department as "The Foghorn" because of his booming voice. Born (1936) in Dicken County, Texas, he was schooled in Richmond, California, and later attended San Jose State College.

Thereafter, armed with a degree in recreation, he worked for the parks department in San Carlos. His initial assignment was teaching young children archery and trampoline. Among numerous achievements at San Carlos was the installation of the first automatic sprinkler system in Northern California.

"I knew Ralph Shaw and Jack Brook and became increasingly interested in the county parks, especially Coyote Point…it was obvious it was going to be the gem of the bay." In 1969, he was hired by Shaw, not for an assignment at the Point but as the first supervising ranger at Sam McDonald Park. For a while, "I didn't have a staff, tools, a telephone, office, or desk."

Emert was the first supervisor to be hired from outside the county. "I brought a different perspective to the department…[M]y professional orientation has always been to get people into parks."

Over the years, Emert served as a ranger at McDonald, Coyote Point, Huddart and Flood parks. In 1973, along with rangers Rich Wilkins and Kendall Simons (the so-called "Three Wisemen" of the department), Emert was appointed Area Manager. Almost single-handedly he was responsible for conducting negotiations for the closure of Sawyer Camp Trail to motor vehicles and its acquisition for park uses.

By 1978, when severe budgetary cutbacks gutted the department requiring the abolition of the position of assistant director and elimination of four chiefs, Emert was the single survivor.

Doc Mattison appointed him Chief of Parks Maintenance and Operations, responsible for the entire 14,000-acre park system. He supervised fourteen county parks, two historical sites, the Coyote Point Junior Museum, and the Coyote Point Marina. In all, reporting to Emert were sixty-four staff members, including rangers, naturalists, gardeners, two area managers, the harbor master, ranger master and all maintenance and construction personnel. "My job was to figure out what needed to be done and then find somebody to do it, or do it myself," he states.

Park reorganization in 1985 resulted in a change of title. Emert became one of two Superintendents of Parks. In 1992, he was placed in charge of Parks Planning and Development.

Before retiring in 1996, Emert had served during the tenure of all park directors except Mary Burns.

Parks Superintendent Bob Emert (right) talks with California plant ecologist Steve Rae at Edgewood Park.

Parks Director David Christy headed the division for a dozen years until retirement in 1993. The effects of his unique style of management are still felt throughout the system.

parks. Emert clearly remembers how he and Mattison spent one afternoon on San Bruno Mountain talking over plans. "We spent a lot of time out there just talking and eating wild blackberries."

Mattison's subordinates knew what was expected of them and that "they had better deliver." He was well-liked, honest, and went to great lengths not to offend anyone — that is, unless he had to. And then, adds Emert, the recipient of his wrath "never recovered." Those who failed to deliver didn't last long. As director, Jack Brook maintained strong loyalty to the old-time park personnel. "My attitude," stated Mattison emphatically, "was you produce or I'll get rid of you."

Doc Mattison had the misfortune of being director in 1978 when the notorious Proposition 13 was passed by California voters. This restriction on property taxes brought about severe budgetary reductions for the parks. "Many of the parks personnel, fearing the absolute worst, simply packed their bags," reports Emert. Mattison was asked to come up with a worst case scenario — how to run the parks with no more than fourteen rangers — one for each of the park units.

Whereas such drastic cuts did not become necessary, Mattison was ultimately forced to get rid of the assistant director position and lay off three of his four leading administrators. In an instant, the entire interpretive staff was eliminated. Before Proposition 13, there were seventy-eight field people; afterwards there were forty.

Proposition 13 was "rough on the director and everybody." The destruction of the department "made Doc sick," declares Emert in retrospect. "It certainly did nothing

for his high blood pressure…" But, concludes Emert, "as a result of Proposition 13, we became a better department. It forced us to mechanize and to do more with less."

David Christy, who graduated from the University of Idaho in forestry management, became director upon Mattison's retirement in 1982. A former U.S. Army artillery officer and previously director of the Santa Clara Parks and Recreation Department, the bright and well-educated, albeit notoriously frugal, Christy brought a new philosophy to the San Mateo department (1982-1993).

"He came at a difficult time and had a philosophy to make hard times work," reports ever-ebullient parks superintendent Lynne Fritz, "David believed that a park was a place for solitude." Rangers were told to reduce services and stay out of the public's way.

The well-groomed Christy, a micro-manager, maintained a high degree of popularity with park commissioners. Kendall Simmons, the department's first African-American administrator, who rose to the rank of Area Manager, states emphatically: "Christy did exactly what the commission asked him to do. His concept was that parks did not need to provide the public with extra services."

That interpretive programs for guests of the parks had been eliminated in the tumultuous backwash of Proposition

13 was not seen as a problem by him. "Christy was the only director I've worked for who did not fight for the budget," adds Emert.

On the other hand, when the suggestion was made that Pescadero Creek Park should be logged for revenue, Christy drew the line. It did not occur.

Under his administration, a ranger's job was to maintain the park, keep it clean, and be invisible. "People go to parks to feel good and don't want to be hassled by rangers," states Christy, now retired and a resident of Boonville, California.

Better economic times accompanied the tenure of parks director Patrick Henry Sanchez (1993-1998) who succeeded Christy. Sanchez, who held a degree in public administration from Long Beach State University with advanced study in park management from the University of California, Davis, came to San Mateo County after five years as director of community services at Oceanside, California. There, he managed 600 acres of parks and almost four miles of coastline.

Superintendent Lynne Fritz speaks well of him. "He was perfect for the time. He believed in communicating and wanted to reach out to the public by supporting a partnership with the community."

Sanchez, who was athletic, quick, and exceedingly bright, recognized the importance of public participation.

During his administration he created the position of volunteer coordinator. Not only was he willing to listen to concerns of parks users but was effective in encouraging them to participate in planning and maintenance.

Mary Burns brought fresh ideas to the division when she came aboard as San Mateo County's first woman director in September 1998. She introduced a regional approach to parks management.

Burns, who grew up in the Central Valley town of Oakdale, California, got her introduction to parks and recreation at the age of fourteen. She volunteered to help in a pre-school "learn to swim" program. Eventually, she became a lifeguard and swimming instructor. "My mother instilled a spirit of volunteerism in me and I enjoyed working with kids."

During summers, she continued as a swimming and playground instructor while a student at San Francisco State University. "But I never thought I would become a parks and recreation person...I assumed I would end up teaching history or political science."

For a year after graduation, Burns worked with the legislature in Sacramento. There she acquired an interest in budgets and their use as policy documents. Perhaps more importantly, Burns developed a comfortable working relationship with elected officials.

Patrick Henry Sanchez served as director briefly before accepting a similar position at the City of Tustin in Orange County.

Mary Burns, a native Californian, became San Mateo County Parks and Recreation Director in 1998.

KENDALL SIMMONS

Although born in Oklahoma City (1940), Kendall Simmons grew up in California. He was the product of Berkeley public schools, attended San Jose City College, and studied recreation administration at Hayward State College.

His first experience in recreation came when he was a teenager. "At thirteen, I went to work for the Berkeley Rec Department at the Grove Street Park Center…handing out balls and planning games for kids…. I enjoyed it and got real satisfaction helping in the African-American community."

Between 1966 and 1973, he was recreation director in East Palo Alto. There he attracted the favorable attention of Jack Brook, San Mateo County Parks Director.

Kendall Simmons was hired as an Area Manager in 1973 and continued in park administration until retirement in 1999.

Brook wanted to introduce ethnic and sexual diversity to his department. Additionally, a former recreation man himself, Brook recruited Simmons for the purpose of revamping recreation programs.

Simmons joined the county in 1973, hired as one of three Area Managers. He was the first African American on the Parks staff and one of the first Black public administrators in the county. Simmons initially had supervisorial responsibilities for Flood and Huddart parks along with Sanchez Adobe. "Jack Brook was my mentor. I also worked closely with Glen Smith, Chief of Recreation…. The assumption was that I'd take over that position when he retired."

But the spector of Proposition 13 and anticipated tax cutbacks changed this career pattern. After 1978, all county recreational programs abruptly ceased.

During a twenty-five-year career with the county, Simmons survived frequent reorganizations. He was gradually elevated to being one of the department's most influential leaders. Early on, he was placed in charge of manpower and budget, safety programs, and entry-level hiring. "I was responsible for hiring every ethnic minority and women working in the department today," Simmons states with pride. Dewayne Austin, the department's first

African-American ranger, presently serving at Flood Park, was hired in 1973.

Pam Noyer, supervising ranger at Flood Park, remembers Simmons warmly. "Unquestionably, as a result of his efforts, this department is today much more receptive to both women and people of color."

When David Christy was director, Simmons acted as his special confidant with responsibility for both hiring and inter-deparmental promotions. "I was virtually an assistant director…Christy always discussed what was going on with me."

Subordinates remember Simmmons as sincere and supportive. "There were always a lot of smiles and 'atta boys' when Simmons came around," remarks Ranger Ron Weaver.

Simmons retired in March 1999. "There were some bumpy spots and a few bad memories but most of the years with the Parks Department were the best of my life," he says. Simmons, however, still cringes when asked about Flood Park's 1987 Cinco de Mayo program. "We expected 800 people; on the day of the event almost 11,000 showed up." The park's 350 parking spaces filled quickly. People were parked for blocks around and, for hours, the neighborhood was gridlocked. Simmons laughs: "That was one of the bumps few have managed to forget."

Sometime later she was hired by San Francisco Mayor George Moscone in policy and budget analysis and, after his assassination, stayed on for a time working with Mayor Dianne Feinstein. Thereafter, she become assistant general manager of the San Francisco Recreation and Parks Department and, in 1985, general manager.

"We had responsibility for 216 park facilities in the city, including Sharp Park Golf Course in Pacifica and Camp Mather near Yosemite." Part of her job was to locate, purchase, and develop new parks in neighborhoods of the city where there were none. These areas included Hunter's Point, Chinatown, and the Tenderloin.

The department also identified and began to restore natural areas on Mount Davidson, Twin Peaks, Bayview Hilltop, and Glen Canyon.

Reflecting on her years in San Francisco, Burns notes that she worked with mayors Moscone, Feinstein, Art Agnos, and Frank Jordan.

Mary Burns became San Mateo County Parks and Recreation Director in September 1998. "My first day on the job was Labor Day," she remarks smiling. "Our issues and problems are different from San Francisco's and our tale to tell is also different."

Burns, who heads a department of sixty field workers and about a dozen in the office, is eminently comfortable with the parks commission and the County Board of Supervisors.

"Mary is extremely effective in marketing the parks," states assistant superintendent Dave Moore. She wants to

develop greater liaison with the county's public schools and to create materials that will assist teachers teaching about the environment. "There are so many things that can be done if we can get the funding to do it," Burns adds.

Upon her appointment, she was delighted to find the San Mateo County Parks and Recreation Foundation already in place. The foundation plays a key role in what the parks are doing. "In the short term, foundation monies are being used for some things that tax dollars usually pay for — playground equipment and the site plan for Sanchez Adobe, for example. Parenthetically, Burns views the foundation as a means to demonstrate that there is broad-based community support for the parks.

Burns singles out the parks' field staff for special commendation. Rangers "are the hidden treasures of the county…they manage to do so much with so little." She comments on their strong commitment to the lands they manage. "Rangers create first impressions with the public and are our ambassadors in the parks." Unlike directors Christy and Sanchez, Burns sees an expanding role for rangers in areas of interpretation, that is, as educators telling the story of the parks.

The soft-spoken director draws attention to the "incredibly rich and diverse parks system that this generation has inherited." She adds that now we "have to have the wisdom to manage it."

Burns is determined that there will be a parks legacy for future generations and that the one we "leave behind should be even better than the one we inherited."

SAN MATEO COUNTY PLANNING DEPARTMENT

Epilogue

San Mateo County parks continue to develop and improve. Today, thanks in large part to ongoing efforts by planners, rangers, and volunteers, many, albeit not all of the ugly scars left by logging operations and other types of unwise land usage common earlier in the nineteenth and twentieth centuries, have begun to disappear. While this job is far from complete, now, in many places, forests and meadowlands have almost miraculously been revitalized.

Dedication of the personnel notwithstanding, the next chapter of this remarkable story rests with those who use and appreciate San Mateo County's many unique parks. The number of citizens who frequent them has risen dramatically over the years, and it is expected that this number will only continue to increase as the population soars.

Indeed, users are the ultimate judges of the parks. Their continued support and cooperation in the common effort to preserve and protect the natural environment will in fact determine the future of these extraordinary places.

PHOTOGRAPH BY SHIRLEY BURGETT

Trillium, a native plant, is found in many of the San Mateo County Parks

Acknowledgments

This history and introduction to park appreciation has been made possible by the San Mateo County Parks and Recreation Foundation. In gathering material and establishing necessary liaisons, the authors worked closely with Julia Bott, the foundation's executive director. Her guidance and assistance made our job not only more pleasant but also far easier.

The authors also wish to thank parks director Mary Burns and her entire staff for their cooperation. With their efforts, normally locked doors miraculously opened, often revealing documents and photographs we would not otherwise have known to exist. For several months park aide Merrilynn Rawstron guided the authors through mountains of documents that have been accumulating in Redwood City for more than half a century. The road map provided by her proved invaluable. Over the years, few government agencies have been more successful in maintaining such thorough records.

Additionally, we have gratitude for historian Eileen Darrah, a person we have neither met nor communicated with. While working for the parks division, during the 1980s, she recorded on audio tape dozens of oral interviews with pioneers of the division. In the interim, many of these people have passed away. As a result of her efforts, we were able to listen to the story of the parks from the pioneers in their own words.

Special thanks are due to longtime parks commissioner Nita Spangler with whom we consulted on an ongoing basis. Her knowledge of parks history and personnel has been invaluable and, over the course of months, saved us days of research.

Darwin Patnode, Ph.D., executive director of the San Mateo County Community College Foundation deserves to be singled out for his technical advice, special assistance, and editorial skills. His efforts contributed to making this a better presentation.

We also want to acknowledge Stephen Haag of Haag 'N Haag Photography on Third Avenue in San Mateo. Through the use of modern computer technology, Haag managed to restore faded or otherwise damaged photographs to their original luster.

Benefactors

The San Mateo County Parks and Recreation Foundation
wishes to express gratitude to the
following individuals and corporations
for their generous support of this publication:

Melvin and Joan Lane

Bohannon Family Foundation

First National Bank of Northern California

and the

County of San Mateo

About the Authors

Michael Svanevik and Shirley Burgett have been writing local history since the mid-1980s. Among their historical credits are thirteen books, including: *No Sidewalks Here—A Pictorial History of Hillsborough, California* (1992), *Burlingame—City of Trees* (1997), and *Menlo Park—Beyond the Gate* (2000). They also wrote *City of Souls—San Francisco's Necropolis at Colma* (1995), and *Class Act—College of San Mateo, a history* (1997).

The pair has produced weekly newspaper columns since 1986 and are now recognized as the premier historical writers on the greater San Francisco Peninsula. Their work appears regularly in the *Peninsula Independent* and the *San Francisco Examiner*. In addition to their monographs, they have written four historical documentaries for television and published almost one hundred magazine articles.

Svanevik, who holds a Master of Arts degree in History from the University of San Francisco, is a professor of Western and local history at the College of San Mateo. Burgett, a specialist in historical research, holds both a degree in History and a Master of Arts degree in Museum Studies from San Francisco State University.

Both authors are native San Franciscans and have been residents of San Mateo County for more than thirty years.

Index

Abalone, 48, 49
Adobe, 19, 20
Adobe House, 46
Alambique Creek, 62, 65
Alambique Flat, 65
Alambique Trail, 63
Alexander, Barbara, 37
Alpine Creek, 76, 79, 80
Alternative Funding Committee, 88
Alvarado, Juan B., 45, 62
Alvarez, Priscilla, 59, 64
American Legion, 12, 13
American Tower Company, 71
Audubon Society, 70
Austin, Dewayne, 96, 97
Australian gum tree, 27
Baker, Tom, 24, 25, 66, 81
Banana Slugs, 86
Band-tailed Pigeons, 5
Bay Checkerspot Butterfly, 57, 58, 69
Bear Gulch Creek, 63
Berglund, Hector, 22
Big Basin, 11
Big Creek Lumber Company, 81
Black-tail Deer, 4, 11, 54, 57, 61, 86
Bloomquist, Henry, 87
Bobcats, 5, 54, 57
Bortolazzo, Julio, 39
Bott, Julia, 88, 89, 91, 100

Bowie Estate Company, 27
Bowie, Henry Pike, 27
Boy Scouts, 13, 14, 37, 61, 78, 83, 87
Breen, Robert, 21, 48, 50, 74
Brock, Charles, 62, 65
Brook, John Jr. "Jack," 21, 22, 81, 91, 93, 94, 96
Brooks Creek, 53
Brown, Arthur Jr., 65
Brown, Charles, 63
Burlingame, 27, 29, 37
Burlingame Railroad Depot, 37, 56
Burns, Mary, 90, 95, 97, 98, 100
Bushnell, Nolan, 65
Byrd, Andy, 37
California, 56, 61, 70, 84
California Employment and Training Act (CETA), 72
California Midwinter International Exposition of 1894, 55
California Native Plant Society, 82
California Poppy, 57, 72, 73
California Sea Otter, 51
Californios, 44, 45
Callippe Silverspot Butterfly, 69
Campbell, Ronald "Ro," 15, 16, 17, 19, 20
Camp Eden, 9
Camp Pescadero, 14
Camp Pomponio, 83
Cañada College, 43
Cangemi, Phyllis, 18
Captain's House, 35

Carol, Jonathan, 65

Chagunte, 42

Chee-Chee-Wa-Wa, 76, 77, 79

Chinese, 26, 63

Christy, David, 24, 25, 70, 94, 97, 98

Cloud, Jean, 90

Cloud, Roy W., 9, 10, 90

Cold War, 73

College of San Mateo, 39

Committee to Save San Bruno Mountain, 70, 71

Consolidation Act of 1856, 63

Coppinger, John, 62, 63

Costanoans, 42

Costeños, 42

Cotogeñes, 42

Coyote Point, 7, 25, 26, 27, 28, 29, 30, 31, 32, 33, 34, 35, 36, 37, 39

Coyote Point Marina, 24, 25, 36, 37, 38, 43, 92

Coyote Point Museum Association, 34, 35

Coyote Point Museum Auxiliary, 35

Coyote Point Museum for Environmental Education, 7, 34, 35

Coyote Point Recreation Area, 7, 24

Coyote Point Rifle and Pistol Range, 36

Coyote Point Yacht Club, 37, 38

Coyote Point Yacht Harbor, 26, 37

Coyotes, 4, 5, 54, 57

Crocker, Charles, 68

Crocker Estate Company, 68

Crocker Land Company, 68, 69, 70, 73

Crystal Springs Dam, 27

Cutler, Fletcher A., 13

Darrah, Eileen, 100

Dean, Harry Jr., 24, 25, 68, 69, 79, 84

Decorators' Show House, 34

Douglas Fir, 2, 60, 79

Durkin, Steven J., 52, 74, 75

Dusky-footed Woodrat, 4

Dyson, Linda, 88

Edgewood County Park and Natural Reserve, 4, 25, 55, 56, 57, 58, 59, 91

Edgewood Hills State College, 56

Emert, Robert S. "Bob," 6, 21, 22, 25, 54, 74, 78, 84, 85, 91, 92, 93, 94, 95

Endangered Species Act, 71

Eshoo, Anna, 71

Fairy Rings, 60, 61

Finkler, Henry C., 55, 56

Fitzgerald, James V., 50

Flood, James, 60

Flood, James C., 17

Flood Park, 16, 17, 18, 19, 20, 21, 22, 23, 88, 89, 96, 97

Flood Park Pool, 19, 20, 22, 23

Flora of San Bruno Mountain, 69

Folger, James A. II, 64, 65, 66

Fort Funston, 73

Fremont, John C., 45

Friends of Edgewood Natural Preserve, 82

Friends of Fitzgerald Marine Reserve, 82

Fritz, Emanuel, 15

Fritz, Lynne Weaver, 74, 94, 95

Fritz, Michael W., 24, 25, 53, 87

Gilley, Jesse, 25, 39, 53, 54

Golden Gate National Recreation Area, 2

Gray Fox, 4, 54

Gray Squirrel, 4, 61

Great Depression, 15, 16

Great Horned Owl, 5

Gumboat Chiton, 51

Haag, Stephen, 100

Habitat Conservation Plan (HCP), 71, 72

Half Moon Bay, 42

Half Moon Bay Band, 13
Half Moon Bay High School, 50
Hanson, Natalie, 9
Harrison Canyon, 9, 10, 12
Hart, John, 61
Hatch, Alvin S., 10
Hays, John Coffee, 63
Hays Ranch, 63
Hazel Wood Farm, 63, 64, 66
Hazelwood Hills, 64, 66
Heritage Grove Redwood Preserve, 80, 81, 86
Hickey, Thomas L., 11, 12, 13, 90
Higgins, Bette, 70
Highway I-280, 6
Hildreth, Elon, 33, 35, 39
Holmes Lumber Company, 80
Hoover, Herbert, 76
Hopkins, Timothy, 10
Hotel San Pedro, 45, 46
Howard, George, 26, 27
Howard, William Davis Merry, 26, 27
Howard, William Henry, 27
Huddart County Park, 3, 5, 59, 60, 61, 62, 82, 96
Huddart, James M., 60, 61
Hunt, Patrick, 55
Ideal Cement Company, 68
Isaac, John, 55
James V. Fitzgerald Marine Reserve, 2, 3, 43, 47, 49, 50,
    51, 75, 82
Japan Air Lines, 38
Jaspar Ridge, 58
Jepson Laurel, 6
Jepson, Willis Lin, 6
Jones, Everett, 64
Jones Gulch, 1
Jones, Simon L., 63, 64, 66

Jordan, David Starr, 77
Junipero Serra County Park, 54
Kamchatka Point, 68
Keaton, Morgan, 13
Kenney, John, 79, 83, 87, 88, 90
Knight, Goodwin J., 77
Knight, Walter, 69
Kuentzel, Kurt, 11, 12
La Honda, 73, 76, 77, 78
La Honda-Alpine-Ytaioa Reserve, 76
Larson, Ellie, 70
Legion Flat, 90
Leidesdorff, William, 45
Liebes, Linda, 35
Light, S.F., 49
Loewe, Frederick, 12
Logging, 3, 5, 8, 10, 15, 40, 41, 60, 63, 80, 81, 83, 84, 85, 86
Lorton, Fred D., 10
Lux, Charles, 8
Madrone, 2, 11, 62
Manzanita, 69
Marchi, John, 38
Martin, William J., 10
Mattison, Duane "Doc," 24, 70, 74, 92, 93, 94
Mattison's Rock, 71
May, Cliff, 19
Mayer, Olive, 24
McClintock, Elizabeth, 69
McDonald, Emanuel B. "Sam," 73, 76, 77, 78, 79
McLaren, John, 25, 27
Memorial County Park, 9, 11, 12, 13, 14, 15, 16, 17, 20,
    21, 22, 86, 87, 88, 89, 90
Memorial County Park Rededication, 89, 90
Memorial-Pescadero Creek Park Complex, 10, 79, 83, 84,
    86, 88
Menlo-Atherton High School, 23

Menlo Park, 17

Milagra Ridge, 73

Miller, Henry, 8

Miller, Jack, 37

Mills, Darius Ogden, 54

Mission Blue Butterfly, 69

Mission San Antonio Padua, 55, 56

Mission San Francisco de Asís, 43

Montara Mountain, 53

Monterey Building, 55

Moore, David, 22, 24, 60, 74, 98

Morris, Charles S. "Jumbo," 32

Moss Beach, 2, 47, 48, 49, 50, 51

Moss Beach Hotel, 48

Moss Beach Marine Reserve, 47

Mountain Dell Division No. 74, Sons of Temperance, 41

Mountain Home Ranch, 63

Mushrooms, 79, 86

National Foundation for Junior Museums, 36

Native Americans, 26, 42, 43, 44, 47, 54, 55, 71

Nike Radar Missile Sites, 73

Noyer, Pam, 89, 97

Nye, Charles, 48

Oaks, 11, 54, 60

Ocean Shore Railroad, 48, 49

Ocean Wave, 28

O'Connor, Tom, 79, 84, 85

Ohlone, 42

O'Leary, Arthur, 38

Oljones, 42

Oracle, 82

Ortega, José, 53

Pacifica, 41, 52, 53

Pacific City, 27, 28, 29

Parkhurst, Mathias, 39, 40

Patnode, Darwin, 100

Paul, Gary, 43

Peninsula AIDS Memorial Grove, 60

Pescadero, 1, 40

Pescadero Creek, 14, 22, 81, 84, 85, 86, 87, 89, 90, 95

Pescadero Creek Park, 25, 83, 84, 85, 86

Peterson, Edwin T., 11

Peterson Lumber Company, 10

Pillar Point, 47

Poett, Agnes, 27

Polar Bear Club, 7, 22

Portolá, Gaspar de, 2, 53

Princeton, 42

Proposition 13, 23, 34, 94, 96

Pruristac, 42

Puma (Mountain Cat), 5

Purisima Creek, 42

Pygmy Owl, 5

Quail, 5, 57

Raccoons, 4

Radwell, Grace Anne, 80

Ramirez, Nick, 82

Rancho Buri Buri, 45, 54

Rancho Cañada de Raymundo, 63

Rancho San Mateo, 26

Rancho San Pedro, 45

Rangers, 74, 75, 98

Rawstron, Merrilynn, 100

Red-shafted Flickers, 5

Red Star Stage Line, 48

Red-tailed Hawks, 5

Redwood City, 40, 55, 56

Redwood City Tribune, 61

Reefs (The), 48, 49

Reichhardt's Duck Farm, 67

Rockefeller, David, 68

Rodgers, Jane, 80

Salamander Flat, 65

Sam McDonald Park, 78, 79, 86, 93

San Andreas Fault, 5, 65

San Bruno, 54

San Bruno Elfin Butterfly, 69

San Bruno Mountain State and County Park, 4, 25, 43,
    58, 66, 67, 68, 69, 70, 71, 72, 73, 82

San Carlos, 21, 22, 93

Sanchez Adobe, 39, 41, 43, 45, 46, 47, 91, 96

Sanchez, Francisco, 44, 45, 46

Sanchez, José Antonio, 44, 45

Sanchez, Patrick Henry, 62, 95, 98

Sand Pirates, 29

San Francisco Bay, 53

San Francisco County, 61, 63

San Francisco Garter Snake, 69

San Francisco International Airport, 7, 38, 68

San Francisco Junior League, 36

San Francisco – Oakland Bay Toll Bridge, 9

San Gregorio, 42

San Mateo (City), 26, 27, 28, 32, 43

San Mateo County, 1, 2, 56, 61, 66, 70, 78, 81

San Mateo County Charter of 1932, 15

San Mateo County Fish and Games Protective
    Association, 85, 86

San Mateo County Historical Association, 41, 46

San Mateo County Horsemen's Association, 90

San Mateo County Junior Museum, 34, 36

San Mateo County Parks and Recreation Department, 5,
    9, 23, 29, 33, 34, 35, 41, 46, 47, 50, 70, 89, 93

San Mateo County Parks and Recreation Foundation, 88,
    89, 90, 91, 98

San Mateo County Planning Commission, 15, 16

San Mateo County Recreation Commission, 15, 16, 91

San Mateo County Sheriff's Honor Farm, 83

San Mateo Fishing Pier, 9

San Mateo – Hayward Bridge, 9, 36

San Mateo Junior College, 32, 33

San Mateo Point, 31, 32

San Mateo Thornmint, 56, 57

San Pedro Creek, 2, 53

San Pedro Valley, 41, 42, 43

San Pedro Valley County Park, 25, 52, 53, 82

San Pedro y San Pablo, 42, 43

Santa Cruz Lumber Company, 83, 84, 85

Santa Cruz Mountains, 1, 5,

Save Edgewood Park Coalition, 58

Sawyer Camp Trail, 5, 6, 93

Schooley, David, 70

Schumaker, William, 24

Scottish Yellow Gorse, 73

Sea Urchins, 51

Sequoia Sempervirens (Coast Redwoods), 1, 8, 9, 20, 43,
    60, 61, 63, 79, 80

Serpentine Rock, 55, 57

Shark Derby, 37

Shaw, Ralph Howard, 20, 21, 22, 23, 24, 32, 33, 36, 38,
    47, 48, 54, 67, 69, 78, 84, 85, 91, 92, 93

Shaw, Rey, 21

Shiga, 38

Shortridge, Samuel, 76

St. Clair, Robert, 35

Serra Fault, 54

Sierra Club, 70, 77

Sierra Morena, 1, 2, 10, 43, 60, 85

Simmons, Kendall, 54, 93, 96, 97

Skunk, 4

Skyline College, 22

Skyline Trail, 62

Smith, Glen, 22, 23, 96

Society for the Prevention of Cruelty to Animals, 75

Sommers, Susán, 58, 59

Southern Pacific Railroad, 56

Spanish Missionaries, 19, 42, 43

Spangler, Nita, 21, 71, 88, 100

Spangler, Ray, 61

Spring Valley Water Company, 27

Ssatumnumo, 42

Stagecoach Service, 5, 40

Stanford Convalescent Hospital, 77, 78

Stanford University, 76, 77, 78

Steelhead Trout, 53, 85

Steller's Blue Jay, 5

Sunset Magazine, 19

Sweeney Ridge, 2, 53

Swing, Warren, 14, 87

Sycylo, Ray, 23

Tanoak, 2

Tarwater Creek, 86

Towne, Kendall B. "Pete," 78

Towne Ridge, 78

Townsend Chipmunk, 4

Trejo, Ricardo, 82

Tripp, Robert Orville, 39, 40, 41

Trout Farms, 52, 53

Truman, Harry, 37

Tuffley, John, 81

Turkey Vulture, 5

Twain, Mark, 68

U.S. Army Signal Corps, 73

U.S. Merchant Marine Academy, 25, 30, 31, 32, 33

University of Santa Cruz, 86

VandenBosch, Marian, 83

Vangene, Kermit, 35

Visitacion Rancho, 68

Volunteer Horse Patrol, 83

Volunteers, 82, 83, 89, 95

Waddell, Helen Hickey, 90

Watson, A.J., 12

Weasels, 4

Weaver, Ronald S. "Ron," 22, 25, 66, 68, 72, 90, 97

Weinke, Juergen F., 48

Werder, Bert, 61

Western Meadowlark, 56

White-rayed Pentacheate, 57

Wieslander, A.E., 1

Wilbur, Ray Lyman, 77

Wildflowers, 55, 57, 58, 72, 73, 86

Wilkins, Rich, 93

Williamson, Josiah C., 10

Wilson, E.O., 67

Wisnom Lumber Company, 27

Wodehouse, Edmund, 53

Woodhams, Gary, 15, 21, 76, 86, 88

Woodside, 40, 41, 59. 60, 65

Woodside Library Association, 41

Woodside Store, 3, 5, 39, 40, 41

Works Progress Administration (WPA), 15, 16, 17, 20

Wright, Bruce, 89

Wunderlich County Park, 62, 63, 64, 65, 66

Wunderlich, Martin, 65, 66

Wurr School, 9